GREAT WAR TOMMY

The British soldier 1914–18 (all models)

COVER ILLUSTRATION:
The Great War Tommy. *(Ian Moores)*

First published in November 2013

A catalogue record for this book is available
from the British Library.

ISBN 978 0 85733 241 7

Library of Congress control no. 2013944255

Published by Haynes Publishing,
Sparkford, Yeovil,
Somerset BA22 7JJ, UK.
Tel: 01963 442030 Fax: 01963 440001
Int. tel: +44 1963 442030
Int. fax: +44 1963 440001
E-mail: sales@haynes.co.uk
Website: www.haynes.co.uk

Haynes North America Inc.,
861 Lawrence Drive, Newbury Park,
California 91320, USA.

Printed in the USA by Odcombe Press LP,
1299 Bridgestone Parkway,
La Vergne, TN 37086.

GREAT WAR TOMMY

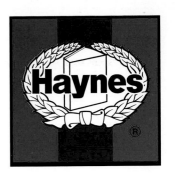

The British soldier 1914–18 (all models)

Owners' Workshop Manual

An insight into the uniform, equipment, weaponry
and lifestyle of the British Great War soldier

Peter Doyle

A soldier of the Essex Regiment pictured in about 1915. Most likely a volunteer of 1914–15, he carries a full set of the stopgap Pattern 1914 leather equipment, and he carries a long Lee-Enfield rifle and bayonet. Nameless, he is typical of so many men who joined the Colours in the early part of the war.

Contents

Introduction

The British Tommy, 1914–18

The First World War continues to fascinate. Despite the views of some revisionists, it is true to say that this most terrible war affected the lives of everyone in Britain and its Commonwealth. For most people living today in Britain, there will be an enduring memory of a family member who lived or died on the Western Front, at Gallipoli or in the Middle East. The First World War is firmly embedded in the school curriculum; year in, year out thousands of schoolchildren cross the Channel to visit the fields of conflict in Belgium and on the Somme. The numbers of people attending the nightly 'Last Post' ceremony at the Menin Gate in Ypres continues to grow, come rain or shine; and, with the release of soldiers' papers at The National Archives, and the availability of the Medal Index Cards online giving details of a soldier's service, there has been a huge growth in family researchers looking for evidence of their relative's time in the armed forces. With the last of Britain's Tommies gone, there is a growing realisation that the First World War will soon be finally committed to history, now that first-hand oral accounts are no longer accessible.

As a consequence of these and other factors, there has been an exponential growth in interest in the British soldier of the First World War period. Most people's imagination is challenged by striking photographs of this war, showing soldiers at rest and in action in their trenches, with hellish images of mud. Yet there is another dimension – that of the equipping and training of the soldier – which is not depicted by these representations of the war. Soldiers devoted much of their service at home, in training or defending these shores; in France or Flanders they spent at least a third of their time away from the trenches. These aspects are largely ignored, yet were a significant component of a soldier's life, and are explored in this book.

There is an abiding fascination in the uniform and equipment of the First World War soldier. What did it feel like to wear? What were puttees for? What did a gas mask look like? How heavy was the equipment? The purpose of this book is to answer some of these questions, and to examine aspects of the training and equipping of the First World War British soldier. Its focus is that of the infantryman, the 'other ranks' soldier equipped and clothed for the Western Front. With the army expanding to a force of almost six million men, there were many specialists, each with their own uniforms and equipment.

There is no room here for the training and equipping of cavalrymen, of specialists such as sappers of the Royal Engineers or the gunners of the Royal Artillery, and it would be impossible to adequately encompass the diversity of roles and responsibilities of the Army Service Corps, for example, or the medical men of the Royal Army Medical Corps, or indeed of officers, with their own uniforms, kit, duties and training. And it would be a major task indeed to give full credit to the men who served overseas in the challenging conditions of Gallipoli, Salonika, East Africa, Mesopotamia and Palestine. Here, in extremes of climate, disease was rife and thirst ever present. In mixed uniforms of khaki drill and serge, Wolseley-pattern sun helmets and 'spine pads' designed to prevent sun stroke, the profile and experience of the British Tommy was very different.

With too great a variation to do these men justice, this book concentrates just on the soldiers of northern Europe. It examines the uniform, equipment and drill of the soldier as set out in the official HMSO-published 'General Staff, War Office' manuals: *Infantry Training (4-Company Organisation), 1914*, published in 1914 and reprinted for every year of the war; *Musketry Regulations Part I, 1909* (reprinted with amendments 1914); its companion *Musketry Regulations Part II, 1910*

(*Rifle Ranges and Musketry Appliances*); and *Field Service Regulations Part I. Operations* and *Part II Organisation and Administration, 1909* (reprinted with amendments 1914). These, and other specialist tomes provide the backbone to a book that seeks to bring some understanding of what it was like to join the army during the First World War. What cannot easily be expressed, however, are the realities of front-line combat conditions, and with them the fear, danger and jeopardy experienced while serving in the trenches, facing death on a day-to-day, hour-by-hour basis. With almost 70% of all First World War casualties being the result of artillery fire, injuries or death could be random and difficult to predict, wounding from artillery fire, trench mortars, grenades, snipers and stray (even spent) bullets adding to the roster. There is no intention to try and represent these features of trench warfare; instead this book is a guide to aspects of the life of the soldier, a means of interpreting soldiers' words preserved in letters, diaries and individual accounts.

Although this volume cannot hope to explore what men felt as they served, it can offer some understanding of those practical matters that were essential to the soldier himself: uniforms and equipment, drill and training, weapons and defences. To this end most of the images used here are of historical interpreters who have researched these facets of the war and through the practice of wearing the uniforms, carrying the equipment and digging the trenches, have some experience of the practicalities of a First World War soldier's life. To gain some idea of the intensity of existence on the Western Front, though, it is necessary to read the actual accounts of the participants – in the books that were produced in the great outpouring of literature that came some ten years after the end of the war, or in the diaries and often halting letters that were sent home by soldiers unable fully to express what they had seen at first hand. With this in mind, this book is respectfully dedicated to the men of the British Expeditionary Force of 1914–18 in the hope that it helps their families appreciate, in some small way, what they had to experience in the defence of their country and of the ideals of freedom.

Acknowledgements

I am grateful to all those who have assisted me in the growth and development of my knowledge of the British soldier of the First World War over many years of study. For this work I am indebted to those historians who have made a practical study of the drill, equipment and training of the British soldier. I am especially grateful to Taff Gillingham of Khaki Devil for access to his storehouse of information and experience – as well as the trenches operated by Khaki Devil Ltd – and to Foz of the Khaki Chums and Neil McGurk of the Durham Pals for their accurate interpretation of the drill movements and exercises carried out by the average recruit in the First World War. My good friend Chris Foster provided much advice and practical support, particularly in the preparation of the photographs in this book. I also thank Keith Bartlett and the Durham Pals, and Peter Zieminski and the men (and machine guns) of the Queen's Own Royal West Kent Living History Group. Ted Peacock, Laurie Milner and Richard Fisher provided access to their First World War collections, and these have enriched my experience. Julie and James are my constant support in all my endeavours; I dedicate this book to them, and to the memory of my loyal friend Luigi, who tragically died while I was writing it.

Chapter One

The First World War and Tommy Atkins

The British soldier had been known as Tommy Atkins for at least a hundred years when he was called to fight in Europe in August 1914. The name stuck with him throughout the war, used by the British people and their enemies alike, and would become associated with stoicism in the most trying of conditions at the Front.

OPPOSITE Soldiers of the Devonshire Regiment pose for the camera, c.1915. They are fully equipped with webbing and SMLE rifles.

The First World War was truly a world war, with campaigns fought by British troops on three continents – Europe, Asia and Africa. For the most part, the Western Front, situated in western Europe, was both to demand most attention and consume in ever-increasing numbers men and materiel. Engaged from August 1914 at the Battle of Mons, the British Expeditionary Force (BEF) grew in size and stature to become the backbone of the Allied effort in the closing months of 1918, in campaigns that defeated Imperial Germany – with 5,399,563 Empire troops employed on the Western Front alone, the vast majority from the UK. Mons (1914), First and Second Ypres (1914), Loos (1915), the Somme (1916), Arras, Messines, Third Ypres and Cambrai (all 1917), the German offensives and Allied advance of 1918, were battles and engagements that were all to take their toll on the BEF – the British armies that served in France and Flanders during the war. But many losses were not the result of battle; instead they were ascribed to 'wastage', the random casualties of war from artillery fire, carelessness in the trenches or from the attention of snipers. Away from northern Europe, British troops were engaged in the costly gamble at Gallipoli in 1915, and in other campaigns against the Ottoman Empire in Mesopotamia and Palestine from 1916. They would face the Bulgarians in Salonika, the Austrians in Italy and the Germans in East Africa. In all, the United Kingdom

would suffer 3,058,985 casualties out of 5,704,416 soldiers enlisted: 724,407 killed; 2,064,451 wounded; and 270,117 missing or prisoners of war.

The British soldier serving in all these theatres of war was known as 'Tommy Atkins', or just 'Tommy' for short. The nickname was at least a century old at the outbreak of war, reputedly selected by the Duke of Wellington himself as a catch-all for the British soldier. Popularised by Rudyard Kipling in the late 19th century, the name was used in official literature, appearing in the pay book as the signature on the standard example of a soldier's will. Universally accepted in the press and in popular songs, the name also found its way across no-man's-land as a counter to Fritz. Though there were other names for British soldiers – such as Jock, for a Scot – it was Tommy that was the most familiar.

When Tommy went to war in 1914, he was part of a small but highly trained army. The army had been overhauled in 1881 by the Cardwell reforms, which created 61 named infantry regiments out of 109 numbered ones, each allied directly with a county or region. Each had a county-based home depot and two, locally recruited, regular battalions. Further reforms by Lord Haldane in 1908 granted regiments a Special Reserve Battalion (whose purpose was to gather recruits), and three locally raised 'Territorial' battalions formed from the volunteer rifle battalions that had been created in the mid-19th century as a means of defending Britain from invasion from the French, a real possibility in 1859. With the threat of invasion having passed, the volunteers had little to do until the Boer War, when they were called to serve overseas; this they did with great verve, earning themselves their first battle honours. With Haldane's reforms these volunteers were transformed into 'Territorial' battalions of regular infantry regiments, part of the Territorial force.

The Territorial battalions had already close allegiances with their local regions, with drill halls located in communities up and down the country providing a means for men to join up and involve themselves in part-time soldiering. Men serving as Territorials did so

DEAR TOMMY,

YOU ARE QUITE WELCOME TO WHAT WE ARE LEAVING. WHEN WE STOP WE SHALL STOP, AND STOP YOU IN A MANNER YOU WONT APPRECIATE.

FRITZ

BATTALION ORGANISATION

From: E. Solano, *Drill and Field Training, 1914*

Infantry battalions in 1914 consisted of around a thousand men organised into four companies (A–D or 1–4). There were four battalions in a brigade, three brigades in a division.

The company. Commanded by a major, with a captain as second in command. Each company was composed of four platoons, numbered consecutively throughout the battalion from 1 to 16.

The platoon. Each platoon consisted of four sections, numbered consecutively through the company from 1 to 16. Each platoon was commanded by a subaltern, with a platoon sergeant as second in command.

The section. The section was the normal fire unit in war; the men who formed it were kept together in the barracks and at the front.

The squad. The term squad was used to encompass a small body of men brought together for drill or fatigue.

LEFT Territorial soldier, a bugler, from the Duke of Cornwall's Light Infantry, c.1914. He wears the 'Imperial Service Commitment' indicating that he had volunteered to serve overseas in times of emergency.

BELOW Imperial Service Commitment badges worn by Territorial soldiers who had volunteered to serve overseas.

on the understanding that they would serve as part-timers engaged on home defence, with no overseas commitment. However, although part-timers, the 'Terriers' were still liable for full-time service on the outbreak of war, the implication being that they would serve at home, while the regulars proceeded overseas. But at the outbreak of war, and the mobilisation of the army, the Terriers were given the option to volunteer for overseas service, those accepting the 'Imperial Service Commitment' entitled to wear a special 'Imperial Service Badge' worn on the right breast pocket. The majority did so; the remainder would lose the right to choose, with the coming of conscription in 1916.

RIGHT Regular soldier in 1914, from the official manual *Infantry Training (4-Company Organisation) 1914*. He is equipped with 1908 Webbing and a Rifle, Short Magazine Lee-Enfield. In October 1914, the left hand cartridge carriers were modified with the addition of extra straps to prevent the loss of cartridges whilst firing in trenches. The model for this illustration had served in the Boer War, as his medal ribbons attest.

RIGHT Recruiting poster from the Parliamentary Recruiting Committee, an all party group committed to assisting the recruitment drive in 1914–15. Like this one, many resorted to emotional blackmail to force men to 'join the colours'.

"BE HONEST WITH YOURSELF. BE CERTAIN THAT YOUR SO-CALLED REASON IS NOT A SELFISH EXCUSE"

LORD KITCHENER

ENLIST TO-DAY

For the regular soldier, mobilised for war, there was the usual budget of training, six months with the third battalion at the base depot before being deployed into the first or second battalion. The regular battalions available at home in 1914 were to form six infantry divisions; each division was to have three infantry brigades – with each brigade in turn composed of four infantry battalions. Brigades rarely had more than one battalion from a given regiment. The typical infantry division of 1914 would also have a significant artillery presence, and an attached cavalry squadron, as well as components from all the other arms and services required to keep it operating in the field, a massive undertaking with up to 20,000 men in a typical, full-strength British division. The six original divisions were to form the British Expeditionary Force (BEF) in 1914, the first four of them taking part in the retreat from Mons in 1914, the other two being present in France by September 1914.

When Field Marshal Earl Kitchener of Khartoum took over as Secretary of State for War in August 1914, he was quick to understand that this war would be costly in manpower. Not confident that the Territorial battalions could be sufficiently flexible to allow rapid expansion, Kitchener made direct appeals to the public, his sights set on increasing the army by 500,000 men, in tranches of 100,000, numbered successively K1, K2, and so on. The first 100,000, or K1, were recruited within days of his request. Kitchener issued four further appeals through the late summer and early autumn of 1914, the final 100,000, K5, being sanctioned by the government in October of that year.

Recruiting offices sprang up across the country, as the demand for men increased. Existing facilities were unable to cope with the throughput of men so local municipal buildings were pressed into service, usually bedecked with banners and posters. On arrival, recruits would be asked their age – 19 being the minimum. It is well known that there were to be very many underage soldiers; the army would later insist that such boys were taken in good faith, having 'lied about their age', and would release them only in exceptional circumstances.

Would-be soldiers were given a brief medical

that assessed physical development and general fitness, based around the height (at first, above 5ft 3in) and chest measurements (34-inch maximum expansion), the condition of the soldiers' teeth (to handle the almost unbreakable ration biscuit), and their eyesight (to be able to sight their rifles effectively). Found fit (categorised A1), recruits would 'attest', involving swearing an oath of allegiance. Signing their forms, they would receive the 'King's shilling', the symbolic issue of the first day's pay of what was to be a long stint in the army. The issue of the shilling, and the repeat of the oath of allegiance to the Crown, would bind the First World War recruit to service for 'three years or the duration of the war'.

With so many men joining the army as private soldiers, more officers were required to command them, and there would be a severe shortfall. Regular officers and NCOs would provide the backbone for the new battalions that were raised following Kitchener's call, but with the demands of regular battalions to be met, manpower resources were tight. Other sources were men on the reserve lists – usually just retired from service, but including more senior men 'dug out' of retirement – together with men on leave from the Indian army. Direct recruitment from public schools and universities was also tried, but as many had joined the ranks as private soldiers it would take some time to persuade them that they might have the skills to command.

The phenomenon most closely associated with the hothouse of recruitment in 1914–15 was the raising of 'Pals' battalions by local dignitaries, 1,000 men strong. Lord Derby suggested the mustering of battalions of men of the 'commercial classes' in a letter published in the Liverpool press on 27 August 1914. The response was dramatic: in just over a week, sufficient men were found for three battalions of 'Liverpool Pals', the fourth being added shortly thereafter. Lord Derby's example was emulated in major towns and cities up and down the country, with varying success. In all, 144 Pals battalions were raised, enough for 12 infantry divisions of the K4 and K5 recruitment tranches.

The first recruits to join Kitchener's New Army were forced to make compromises: little in the way of equipment, no uniforms and no

ABOVE The King's Shilling: the recruit who received his, on 15 November 1915, kept his first day's wages as a keepsake, transformed into a watch fob.

LEFT A corporal of the Durham Light Infantry stands to attention; he wears a uniform typical of 1915–16. NCOs were the backbone of the new army.

LEFT A recruit with Kitchener's Army, c.1914. With khaki serge in short supply, Kitchener's volunteers had to make do with a variety of uniforms finished in blue serge.

barracks. In the early stages of the war, the supply of arms, uniform and equipment to the enthusiastic recruits was a difficult task; the Kitchener battalions were fed, housed and equipped at the initial expense of the authority that raised them. This meant sourcing uniforms from official and even commercial suppliers at a time when the country was alive with such pleas along its length and breadth. As a consequence, recruits were more often than not clothed in civilian garb, and later in a variety of uniforms finished in blue serge that were collectively known as 'Kitchener blue' garments. And as training camps had not yet been formed or established, Kitchener's men found themselves still living at home.

The flow of volunteers decreased steadily month –on month in 1914–15, and the War Cabinet became increasingly concerned that the British army would not be able to withstand its losses at the front. The National Registration Act introduced in July 1915 required every citizen between the ages of 15 and 65 to register their name, place of residence, nature of work and other details. By October 1915, registration had identified 5,158,211 men of military age, with at least 3.4 million technically able to join the forces, but who had not yet volunteered. Lord Derby, appointed Director of Recruiting in 1915, drew up a scheme entailing the voluntary registration, or attestation, of all men between 18 and 40. This legal undertaking to serve only when needed was meant to be a draw, attested men wearing a khaki armband. The scheme failed. The Military Service Act of January 1916 followed, announcing conscription for all fit single men between the ages of 18 and 41, the first of five such acts during the war. Conscripts would make up the majority of the army that marched to victory in 1918.

Starting from an initial number of just six regular divisions (1st–6th) in 1914, the War Office assembled a further 59 divisions throughout the war: 6 regular, 30 New Army,

ABOVE, LEFT AND BELOW Recruits to the Durham Light Infantry (DLI) being put through their paces. The DLI had fifty-three battalions of various types during the war, including regulars, territorials, service battalions, home service battalions and training battalions.

LEFT Soldier of the Army Service Corps attached to the 29th Division, c.1917. He wears the divisional sign of a red triangle – actually meant to be a 'half-diamond' – on each shoulder. This was devised by Lt-General de Lisle, who wished to remind his troops of the importance of the diamond formation in battle.

15 first-line Territorial (composed of soldiers who had signed the Imperial Service Obligation in the first instance), 14 second-line Territorial, 1 Yeomanry Division, 3 Home Service Divisions and 1 compiled from Royal Naval reservists – the Royal Naval Division. Of this total of 75 available divisions, 65 would actually see action overseas. Each division was made up of almost 20,000 men, with the infantry forming the greatest number, comprising, in the early part of the war, some 12,000 men divided between three infantry brigades, in turn composed of three infantry battalions each. In addition, an infantry battalion was attached to the division designated as the 'Divisional Pioneers' – soldiers who in addition to carrying a rifle, would have to wield a pick and shovel. The remainder were composed of the fighting arms such as the artillery and engineers (making up some 5,000 men), and the services, such as the Army Service Corps, which were required to supply the needs of the division in the field, and the cavalry.

The first six divisions had landed in France by mid-September 1914 – though the first four landed there on 17 August – a triumph of preparation and organisation. The remaining regular divisions had crossed to France by January 1915 (though the last to be formed, the 29th Division, was sent to Gallipoli). The initial first-line Territorials followed in February 1915; eight of these divisions were sent to other theatres, such as Egypt, Palestine or Gallipoli, although most were in the field by August 1915. For the New Army men, training and assembly meant that they would have to wait some months before they could be committed to action. The first New Army divisions sent overseas were the 9th (Scottish) and 14th (Light) Divisions, arriving in France and Flanders in May 1915; with four divisions committed to other theatres (Gallipoli and Egypt), the remainder would transfer to France in the latter part of 1915 and into the spring of 1916 – ready to be committed to the coming offensive on the Somme, in July 1916. The last divisions to go were the second-line Territorials – formed originally from men who had signed on only for home service, but who, with the advent of the Military Service Act in 1916, were compelled to comply with the wider regulations from May 1916.

With so many units in the field by 1916–17, an effective system of identifying units as components of a larger formation was needed, for use on the transport, headquarters and men themselves. Left largely to the whim of the commanders of these units, a series of identifying badges was developed that could be painted on battalion transports and the like. Often colourful, these generally referred to the

regional origin of the formation, like the thistle of the 9th (Scottish) Division, the red dragon of the 38th (Welsh) Division or the red rose of the 55th (West Lancashire) Division; or they used a symbol that indicated the number or origin of the division – like the bantam cock of the 40th Division, modified with the addition of an acorn to commemorate the capture of Bourlon Wood on the Somme in 1916, or the broken spur of the 74th Division, composed largely of dismounted Yeomanry troops. Others would be more obscure: the dot and dash of the 17th Division (representing the top of the number 17), for example. Later in the war, cloth versions of these badges would be sewn to the upper sleeve of the service dress (SD), and an even more complex system of brigade and battalion cloth signs would find their way on to the uniform.

FORMATION SIGNS

Formation signs were first devised in about 1916 as a means of distinguishing divisional transport and headquarters, while being obscure to enemy observation and interpretation. For this reason, although some signs are clearly regional in their references, others are geometric symbols, anagrams or emblems indicative of the commander's name, or even just simply chosen at random. The formation signs illustrated were worn on soldiers' uniforms.

Typical late-war formation signs

Top left: 74th (Yeomanry) Division, with symbolic broken spur, a cavalry division transformed into infantry; top right: 55th (West Lancashire) Division, signified by the red rose of Lancashire, and with five leaves on each branch indicating the number of the division; bottom left: 21st Division, made up of three sevens, the total equal to the divisional number; bottom right: 9th (Scottish) Division, its origins made apparent by the use of the thistle, in white metal.

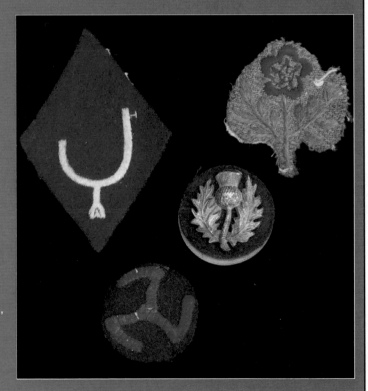

Chapter Two

Equipping and training a First World War Tommy

The British soldier went to war equipped with some of the best equipment, and certainly the best rifle, of any nation. With the expansion of the army from its regular core, supplying sufficient uniforms and equipment was a mammoth task – as was ensuring that the novice soldiers were trained to take on a determined enemy.

OPPOSITE Cleaning the Mark III Short Magazine Lee-Enfield (SMLE), the standard weapon of the British infantryman.

UNIFORM ISSUE, INFANTRY OF THE LINE,* 1914

Personal clothing	
Boots, ankle, pairs	2
Cap, service dress	1
Drawers, woollen, pairs	2
Frock, canvas	1
Jacket, service dress	2
Puttees, pairs	2
Shoes, canvas, pair	1
Trousers, canvas, pairs	1
Trousers, service dress	2
Waistcoat, cardigan	1
Public clothing	
Coat, great, dismounted, men	1
Necessaries	
Badges, collar, pair	1*
Badge, cap	1
Bag, kit, universal	1
Blacking, tin	1
Braces, pair	1
Brushes	
Blacking	1
Brass	1*
Clothes	1
Hair	1
Polishing	1
Shaving	1
Tooth	1
Button, brass	1*
Cap, comforter	1
Comb, hair	1
Disc, identity, with cord	1
Fork	1
Gloves, worsted, pairs	1
Holdall	1
Housewife	1
Knife, clasp, with lanyard	1
Knife, table	1
Mineral jelly, tin	1
Razor	1
Shirts, flannel	3
Socks, worsted, pairs	3
Sponge	1
Spoon	1
Titles, metal, for shoulder-straps, with grenades for fusilier and bugles for light infantry regiments, sets	3
Towels, hand	2

*Non-Highland regiments   **Not for rifle regiments
Regulations for the Clothing of the Army, Part 1 Regular Forces, 1914

In 1914–15, camps were set up across the country to house the vast influx of new recruits to the armed forces; they would vary considerably from villages of bell tents to timber-constructed huts. On arrival, recruits were issued with their uniforms and equipment; in many cases this would take time, dependent upon the arrival of new stocks of equipment, and often relying upon old, out-dated or obsolete kit. The War Office *Regulations for the Clothing of the Army, Part 1 Regular Forces, 1914*, published just two months before the outbreak of the war, listed the uniform items and 'free kit' – the 'necessaries' that were to be issued to and carried by the average soldier in wartime. The range of items would vary as the war deepened; soldiers would be expected to look after their kit carefully or suffer the consequences of fines or other punishments.

But the creation of an efficient soldier did not rely solely upon the issue of uniform; with the army keen to mould civilians into efficient fighting men there was a full programme of training – training that was intended to create a fit body and calmness under fire. With many civilians, fitness was an issue, and the application of a simple regime of physical education – involving the application of the Swedish drill system of 'physical jerks' – together with long runs and the use of route marches in full equipment, would be essential. Fitness was accompanied by lectures and a syllabus of training in the use of a soldier's personal weapons, as well as ceremonial drill, this last intended to create automatic discipline, and therefore calmness under fire. For those unused to such exercise this was a new and challenging experience, the basis for the transition from civilian to soldier, the foundation of his new life as a man serving in the front line facing a determined foe.

Clothing the soldier

The khaki uniform worn by the British soldier was first developed in 1902 as a replacement for the traditional red coat of the British infantryman, still in active service during the Imperial 'small wars' of the late 19th century. A cotton service dress of khaki was in full use in the Boer War of 1899–1902, and the success of this, blending effectively with the dusty landscape, led to the development of the wool serge version used by Tommy that would survive, with modification, into the early part of the Second World War. This new uniform was designed to suit all purposes; when the army put its ceremonial red coats into storage at the outbreak of world war, it would be some time before they were seen again.

The 1902 pattern service dress, the standard uniform of the British First World War soldier, was the product of a basic military requirement to have comfortable and serviceable clothing that would be suited for field conditions, in all weathers. A wool serge uniform was produced that was to be embodied in Army Orders in 1902 as service dress. This garment went through several modifications in the 'Lists of Changes' issued periodically by the War Office,

LEFT Soldier of the Royal Fusiliers wearing standard issue 1902 pattern Service Dress and stiff 1905 pattern cap. He wears the belt while 'walking out'.

BELOW Wartime 1902 Pattern Service Dress jackets. Left to right: Private in the Norfolk Regiment; Corporal in the Honourable Artillery Company, with regimental pattern buttons and single blue overseas service stripe, awarded for each year of service spent overseas; Staff Sergeant in the Royal Inniskilling Fusiliers, with brass titles and two years overseas service; Staff Sergeant in the Royal Field Artillery, with signal instructors flags, regimental arm badges (field guns) and a single 'wounded' stripe on the left arm.

RIGHT Soldiers were commonly photographed in uniform at their base before proceeding overseas, and then again while serving in France. The difference between such photographs is often very distinct, with a more relaxed 'active service' look. This photo shows a soldier of the Royal Fusiliers wearing the simplified pattern service dress jacket and soft cap, c.1916. Simplified pattern jackets were often poorly fitting. The inverted chevron on his left sleeve indicates two-years good conduct in the army.

but by 1914 had settled down to a pattern that was used more or less throughout the war.

The wartime service dress tunic was intended to be loose fitting, with a turned-down collar, patches at the shoulder to bear the extra wear from the position of the rifle butt in action, and pleats to provide a good fit to the rear of the jacket. It had a pair of box-pleated

RIGHT Service Dress trousers.

patch pockets with button-down flaps at the upper chest, and a pair of deep pockets let into the tunic skirt, again with button-down flaps. A simple pocket was also sewn into the inside right skirt of the tunic to take the soldier's first field dressing – the emergency bandages carried by all soldiers on active service. Two brass hooks, often removed or lost through use, were intended to support the webbing belt in its correct position between the sixth and seventh tunic button. For the most part, these buttons were simple brass ones – known as General Service or 'GS' buttons – bearing the royal arms; some regiments insisted upon men buying and replacing these with regimental-patterned examples. The jackets of rifle regiments in particular had black horn buttons that were further distinguished by a bugle. Shoulder straps bore regimental insignia in the form of brass shoulder titles, but a range of other emblems were also used. Throughout the war these were added to the sleeves, including rank badges, specialist trade and appointment badges and divisional insignia.

In late 1915, with the War Office suffering the pressure of large numbers of men coming into the army, a simplified version of the service dress was introduced that dispensed with the rifle patches at the shoulders, the pocket box pleats, the rear fitting pleat to the tunic, and the brass belt hooks. This style was never in favour, and although worn throughout the war, it was replaced with the standard 1902 pattern as soon as was practical. Both types of unlined service dress were worn in the trenches, however, their woollen jackets warm but rough, worn over a series of under-layers. Starting with woollen underwear and a long flannel shirt, in cold weather the jacket was worn over a woollen cardigan. Early on, the soldier's kit also included the so-called body-belt, an incongruous knitted tube that was to be worn over the abdominal region to 'protect the kidneys' from cold; more often than not this was home to lice. In addition, woollen mufflers, socks, balaclava helmets and a host of other small items knitted at home were worn, articles that became the staples of many parcels bound for the front.

Accompanying the jacket was a pair of trousers finished in wool serge and, as was common in the day, they were high waisted. Service dress trousers were quite close fitting, with a narrow leg that was designed to be worn with puttees, while mounted soldiers wore breeches tightly laced over the calves. Both garments were worn with braces, although soldiers often used belts in addition, some personalised with collections of badges and buttons; other types were 'money belts' – privately purchased items with pouches to hold the soldier's pay.

The puttees worn with service dress trousers were a concept derived – like khaki service dress itself – from the British experience in India; the term 'puttee' had its origin in a Hindi word that meant 'bandage'. Puttees were intended to provide a covering for the lower leg that would give support and protection, and that would prevent grit and dirt from entering boot tops. They were also a military fashion of the day, as puttees were used by most nations during the war; in extremis, puttees could also be used to support stretchers, or even a wounded man seated on the back of the soldier carrying him. Learning how to tie the puttee soon became a badge of the experienced soldier. Consisting of long wool serge strips provided with cotton tapes, puttees were wound around the leg from the ankle to the knee for the average infantryman. Mounted soldiers (including cavalrymen, artillerymen and Army Service Corps men, among others) were distinguished by their practice of winding the puttee from the knee to the ankle, the tapes wound close to the ankle. Finding ways of exerting their own personality, soldiers would also create fancy patterns with their puttees, using judiciously applied folds.

During the war, the traditional East Midlands centre of shoemaking, Northampton, was to be stretched to capacity in supplying boots; not only for the British army, but also for most of the Allies in the field, employed on all fronts. During peacetime alone, some 245,000 pairs of boots were required annually to supply the British army. The 'regulation' British field boot for most of the war was roughly square-toed, produced in thick hide with the rough side out. Soldiers issued with the boots for field use were instructed to pack the rough leather with dubbin in order to create a more water-

WINDING PUTTEES

For dismounted men (that is, most infantrymen), puttees were wound from the ankle to the knee. Starting with the puttees rolled so that their tapes appeared last, each puttee was wound gradually around the leg so that the bottom of the puttee cloth covered the boot top. In order to ensure this covering was efficient, each puttee was wrapped around the boot top twice before gradually moving up the calf. In most cases, puttees moulded with age to the leg, the wool material stretching with time. Fitting the puttees took time, as unevenly fitted and unwound puttees looked untidy and unlikely to pass muster on parade. At the top of the leg, the puttee terminated with its tailored point on the outside of the leg, pointing to the rear; to achieve this, often another wind of the puttee was required. The tapes were then neatly coiled around the top, with the end of the fitted puttee tucked under the tape and wound around it so that it did not unravel or fray. Both legs should match in this way.

resistant material, and this produced the tan colour that is so typical of the field boot. The standard pattern early in the war was the 'B2' (first introduced in 1913); the later 'B5' boot, distinguished by its distinctive quarters and copper rivet, saw widespread introduction in 1915–16. Other footwear used by Tommy on the Western Front was the high boot of the mounted artilleryman, and the so-called 'trench waders', made by the North British Rubber Company in Scotland, and centrally held as 'trench stores'.

In 1914, British soldiers went to war in a peaked cap that had been adopted in 1905. This was not designed to protect the head from anything other than the elements, and had a stiffened rim and peak, bearing the traditional regimental cap badges of the British army. The stiffness of this headgear made it awkward, although the stiffening wire in the crown of the cap was often removed in an attempt to soften its profile. Then, in late 1914, an answer to the impracticality of this headgear was the issue of the winter service dress cap, which was well padded and equipped with flaps to keep the ears warm. Ungainly, the mythology is that this cap, which became known as a 'gor'blimey', was so nicknamed by the first sergeant major who cast his eyes upon one – the term deriving from cockney slang for 'God blind me'. Both stiff and winter service dress caps became superseded once the steel helmet was first issued, towards the close of 1915. In its place, was the issue of a soft and practical cap in March 1916 that was capable of being folded and stowed in the soldier's equipment, as it had no stiff components; a stitched peak was the only concession to smartness. Tommy often personalised it by plaiting the leather strap,

CAPS

The caps illustrated show the distinct difference in profile of the standard 1905 pattern service dress cap, and the

BELOW The 1905 pattern stiff cap.

later serge soft cap, introduced following the first issues of the steel helmet in 1915–16. The 1905 pattern had a wired brim and spring to maintain its stiff front; it had a firm, short peak backed with green card material. In some cases, the

FAR LEFT Soldier of the Yorkshire Regiment with well-tied puttees, standard Service Dress and stiff 1905 pattern cap. He carries a stick as a photographic prop, and wears his own, non-army issue boots, as well as the belt from the 1914 leather equipment set.

LEFT Soldier of the Army Service Corps wearing the Winter Service Dress Cap. He is equipped with components of the 1903 Bandolier equipment set.

wire stiffener was removed to create an 'active service' look. The soft cap was distinguished by its absence of rigid components: no internal wires and no peak stiffener. This cap could be easily folded and carried in the pack while the soldier wore his steel helmet; comfortable to wear, this cap was often adapted to suit the style of the wearer.

BELOW The soft 'trench' cap.

25

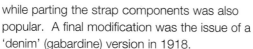

while parting the strap components was also popular. A final modification was the issue of a 'denim' (gabardine) version in 1918.

With the profile of most British soldiers looking broadly the same throughout the war, it was left to the Scots to cut a dash with their distinctive form of Highland dress. Many Scottish regiments were kilted, the kilt warm to wear with its many folds of woollen tartan, but the downside of the folds being their propensity to harbour lice, as well as their ability to soak up vast amounts of water, adding to the weight burden of the average soldier. The bright colours of some regimental tartans was also a problem, such that, by 1915, the kilt was covered by a wrap-around simple apron of khaki cloth. The Scottish service dress jacket was also special: its front skirts were trimmed back in the manner of a traditional doublet to allow the wearing of the full-dress sporran – in some cases by the simple expedient of cutting the corners off his standard SD tunic.

To complement the appearance of the Highland soldier, there were a range of caps and bonnets. In the early part of the war the commonest was the glengarry, found in a variety of patterns: plain dark blue with a red tuft or 'tourie' (worn by the Black Watch and Cameron Highlanders); rifle green with a black tourie (the Cameronians and Highland Light Infantry); red and white diced border and red tourie (Argyll & Sutherland Highlanders); and finally red–green–white diced borders with red tourie (Royal Scots, Royal Scots Fusiliers, King's Own Scottish Borderers, Seaforths and Gordons). There were other regiments who adopted the glengarry too: the territorial 10th Battalion of the King's Liverpool Regiment, the Liverpool Scottish, wore the red–white–green diced border, while the Kitchener's Army battalions of the Northumberland Fusiliers, known as the Tyneside Scottish, adopted a plain black glengarry with red tourie and black silk rosette. Impractical in the field, the glengarry would be replaced in 1915 by first the beret-like balmoral bonnet, and then the serge khaki tam-o'-shanter, a large, circular but otherwise shapeless cap that nonetheless distinguished the Scot.

The standard cold-weather protection issued to the average soldier was the greatcoat, a cumbersome wool serge coat, with a single row of brass GS buttons that weighed in at around 6lb, a considerable amount even when dry. Expensive to manufacture, the greatcoat was also a hefty responsibility for the ordinary soldier, who was expected to look after it – on pain of being fined a significant sum of money. In fact, greatcoats were more often left with the large pack that was issued as part of their equipment and kept with the battalion transport, with other means of keeping the body core warm provided. The first of these was the outlandish (and often multicoloured) goatskin sleeveless jerkin issued in late 1914 that was to see action well into 1916. Worn with the fur side out, these malodorous garments were nevertheless a means of keeping the trunk warm. Goatskins were replaced in 1915 onwards with hard-wearing sleeveless leather jerkins, lined with wool serge and having leather 'football' buttons. Worn both over and under the tunic, these provided warmth and protection, and were much favoured. But shielding from the wet weather of Flanders was entrusted to the issue groundsheet, a rectangular sheet with eyelets that, from 1917 onwards, was modified so that it was provided with a collar and buttons, such that it that could be fastened up to the neck to create a cape, essential while on 'sentry go' in the rain.

With sniping a constant menace, steel helmets were an innovation intended to combat its effects, and to reduce the head injuries that were all too prevalent among men living and working in ditches close to head height. Up until 1915, Tommy wore the service dress cap in all its forms in the front line. In action, this meant that head wounds were common, especially in its static phases when the attention of snipers

LEFT Goatskin and 'gor' blimey' cap.

was concentrated on the movement of soldiers past loopholes and dips in the trench sides. Soldiers were vulnerable to snipers, but they were also subject to the random tragedies of spent bullets, and from air-burst shrapnel and shell fragments. Clearly there was a need for increased head protection, and this was to be introduced in late 1915, with the French, Germans and British producing markedly different steel helmets.

The British steel helmet was designed in 1915 by John Leopold Brodie, an engineer.

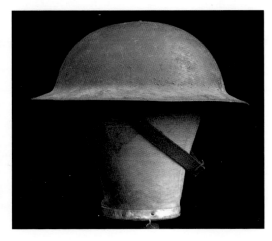

LEFT British Mark 1 steel helmet. The distinctive profile of the British soldier was defined by this dish-shaped helmet, intended to give protection from shrapnel balls and bullets while in the trenches. The 'Mark 1' replaced the 'War Office Pattern' in 1916.

27

RIGHT Brodie's Patent, War Office Pattern helmet showing the exterior and interior with its simple liner and buckled chin strap. This first pattern helmet is distinguished by its raw edge and distinctly apple green paint, often over-painted.

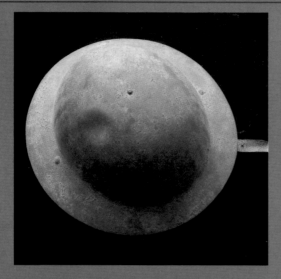

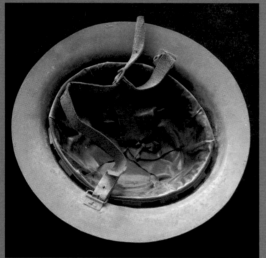

The Brodie-patent helmet went through a few changes following its introduction in 1915, the majority in relation to its liner – always considered to be of the greatest importance by John Brodie himself. The three main changes were:

War Office pattern, March 1915–June 1916: Sharp rimmed helmet; liner with six 'American cloth' tongues laced together in centre, headband with rubber tubes and felt liner; two-part leather chin strap with a tongued buckle.

Mark I steel helmet, June 1916 onwards: Helmet shell now with added mild steel rim; it was fitted with a liner of two parts – a pad attached to the crown of the helmet, and the main section made out of American cloth, consisting of head support and drawstring net. The chin strap had two parts, one that connected with the interior of the helmet, and the chin strap proper, with a sliding buckle.

Mark I steel helmet, modified liner, January 1917 onwards: A rubber ring was inserted in the crown pad in order to give increased protection to the crown.

RIGHT Interior of the later Mark 1 helmet showing the original liner (left) and the liner with rubber crown ring (right).

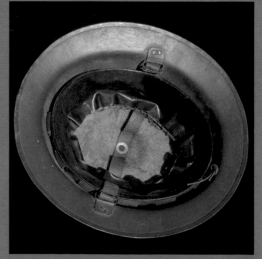

Brodie proposed a simple, easy to manufacture, dish-like helmet that could be punched from a single sheet of steel, with a liner that would resist impact. The liner, granted a patent on 16 August 1915, was an innovative part of the original design, acting 'as a buffer to prevent concussion of the brain by external impact and to prevent injury to the frontal, parietal or occipital bones of the cranium by any indentation or penetration of the helmet'. The shape of the helmet, with the bowl and extended rim, was designed to resist at least spent bullets, as well as shrapnel falling from above, the wide rim deflecting low-energy impacts. Its shell was originally made from mild steel, but this was soon replaced with much harder, non-magnetic manganese steel; its liner was composed initially of a crown pad of felt with lint layers, with a headband containing 12 tubular rubber spacers, all intended to lessen impact. After some trials, the helmet was adopted on 24 September 1915; the production helmet liner was marked 'Brodie's Steel Helmet, War Office Pattern Patent 11803/15'. By March 1916, 270,000 of the original War Office pattern helmets had been produced, with some 140,000 destined for the Western Front. It was battle tested in the Ypres salient and was a success; over one million were supplied to the army by July 1916 – in time for the Battle of the Somme.

The helmet underwent modification as the war progressed. The initial War Office pattern was issued with a sharp, unprotected rim. Problems with the sharpness of its rim, and the smooth reflective surface of the helmet (and complaints to that effect from General Plumer), led to the introduction of an improved helmet, known as the Mark I in September 1916, which had a steel protective rim added, and a non-reflective sand finish. The original helmet liner, and its buckled chinstrap, were also replaced. Brodie continued to improve the liner to ensure that impacts would not be fatal; there were also local modifications, and privately purchased liner options for officers. In most cases, the distinctive silhouette of the 'tin hat', easily picked out by snipers, was disguised by sacking or sandbags in close-fitting covers; some battalions painted divisional signs or attached regimental badges to their helmets or covers.

Equipping the soldier

With quartermasters having difficulties supplying the uniform needs of a greatly expanded army, it is not surprising that they were faced with an even bigger crisis when it came to military equipment. In fact, the provision of appropriate load-bearing equipment has been a question that has taxed the military mind every since the role of infantryman was first conceived. For centuries, the design of equipment – to include ammunition carriers, haversacks for accoutrements, ration carriers, and so on – has centred on the belt, with shoulder straps and braces designed to spread the weight.

Prior to the introduction of the 1908 webbing equipment that was standard for the First World War soldier, the infantry were issued with the 1903 pattern bandolier, introduced in the wake of the Boer War to replace the cumbersome and inadequate Slade-Wallace equipment set. The 1903 set had as its central feature a 50-round leather bandolier that was designed to cross the chest from left shoulder to right hip, looping around a plain leather belt with an open-frame tongued buckle. The full set included a water bottle cradle and strap, also crossing the chest, together with a haversack and strap. Four individual 15-round cartridge pouches were carried on the belt, as was the mess tin, its cover looping over it at the rear. The whole was kept together with straps that held the greatcoat, and which linked two of the cartridge pouches with the mess tin. Complex, time-consuming to assemble, and constricting, during the First World War the 1903 pattern equipment was used only by Territorials, by some men in training, and elements of it by mounted troops.

Fortunately, the 1903 pattern was a short-lived experiment, and its replacement employed a more equable system of weight distribution, a collaboration of military ideas and manufacturing innovation. The 1908-pattern web infantry equipment that replaced it was the ideal: the official guide praised its versatility, its balance, its flexibility, and its lack of constricting chest straps. All of these made the equipment easy to wear and fit for purpose, which meant that soldiers would discard other patterns in its favour, wherever possible.

1903 BANDOLIER EQUIPMENT: 'MARCHING ORDER'

Information from: *Instructions for Fitting and Wearing the Equipment, Bandolier Pattern 1903* (1904)

1 *Front view*

The bandolier crosses the chest, with the water bottle cradle and strap also crossing in the same direction, placing considerable constriction; the haversack is carried across the chest from right shoulder to left hip. The haversack contains the soldier's 'necessaries'. The four cartridge holders are seen attached to the plain leather belt; two of them are top opening and are equipped with brass rings; the straps of the greatcoat carrier connect with these via brass hooks.

2 *Right view*

The greatcoat is rolled in its carrier, and connects with the mess tin set, fastened on the belt. The 'mineral jelly tin' carrier can be seen to the rear; this contains the rifle cleaning kit and pull-through.

3 *Rear view*

The complexity of the equipment set is displayed here, with the greatcoat in its simple webbing strap carrier, attached to the mess tin, and the cross straps of the bandolier, water bottle cradle and haversack.

4 *Left view*

The bandolier is carried under the shoulder strap, together with the greatcoat carrier; the haversack, crossing from the opposite shoulder, can be seen obstructing the bayonet, which is carried in a plain leather frog, suspended from the belt.

Part of the success of the 1908 equipment lay with its greatest innovations; designed by Major Burrowes of the Royal Irish Fusiliers in 1906, it was a complete 'system'. Its thick woven cotton strapping (invented by the Mills equipment company in the United States in the late 19th century) had many advantages over leather. Leather was a cumbersome material difficult to keep clean, and was liable to stretching when wet, characteristics that were not ideal in military equipment. According to the official manual, *The Pattern 1908 Web Infantry Equipment* (1913), the cotton used in constructing the webbing was specially waterproofed before it was dyed, the effect of which treatment was 'to render the material practically impervious to the weather, which might otherwise have tended to make it hard or cause it to stretch and shrink'. To prevent fraying, the webbing straps were finished with riveted brass ends that also allowed the component pieces to be easily fitted together – but which also provided the army with something else for its soldiers to polish until gleaming (though not while in the front line). Corresponding to these straps were tongueless buckles, finished in heavy-gauge brass: the free end of each strap was designed to pass through the slot of the relevant buckle, over the central bar and under the 'horns' to its other side. The open horns meant that it was possible to pinch the strap in order to both fit it in and remove it, pulling the strap through the open slot.

The full 1908 set consisted of belt, cross straps, left and right cartridge carriers (designed to carry 150 rounds in 10 pouches, each holding 3 5-round chargers), water bottle, bayonet frog and entrenching tool (actually an *intrenching* tool to the War Office) in its webbing head carrier. Press studs were used to close the cartridge carriers, although by the end of the war, as an economy measure, the press studs were replaced by post and hole fasteners. Innovatively, the helve for the entrenching tool was strapped to the scabbard of the bayonet. In addition, there was a small haversack, and large pack, with cross-straps to keep the pack in place and balanced. This was achieved by the action of the support of the cartridge carriers in front, balancing the weight at the back; previous equipment sets had the

LEFT Soldier equipped with 1908 equipment and SMLE rifle, c.1919.

BELOW The 1908 belt, front and back.

BOTTOM The 1908 pattern cartridge carriers. In October 1914, the left-hand cartridge carriers were fitted with additional straps to prevent the loss of cartridges when soldiers leaned against trench sides to fire.

Information from: *The Pattern 1908 Web Infantry Equipment* (1913)

Assembling the 1908 equipment set.

The waist belt is adjusted to the body so that it is reasonably tight, and with the buckles central to the belt at its rear. The belt is then laid out, inside downwards, with the large buckle to the right. The bayonet frog is then passed over the belt so that it is on the left-hand side, with the helve carrier strap buckled to it. The carriers are fixed to the belt using double hooks that pass over and under the belt; when an accurate position has been found on the belt, the securing straps to the rear are fastened in position. The braces are then fixed to the rear buckles of the belt, the loose strap matching that on the rear of the belt; and at the front the braces are joined to the buckles at the top of the cartridge carriers, the straps passing behind them and matching the attached straps at the front of the carriers. The haversack is joined to the two outer strap ends on the left-hand side of the belt and fixed into position over the bayonet and helve. In normal circumstances, the entrenching tool carrier is fastened to the right side, fixed to the two inner strap ends. The water bottle carrier is then connected to the right side, using the two outer strap ends. This part-assembled set is known as 'Marching Order equipment without pack'.

The pack is attached by laying the equipment face downwards, the pack placed upwards upon it. The supporting straps are

buckled to the diagonal straps from the rear of the cartridge carriers, the straps going through the loops at the base of the pack and passing diagonally across it to link to the buckles at the top of the pack itself. Finally, the sliding buckles on the brace straps are moved so that they line up with the securing tabs on the pack, the tabs being passed through the buckles to secure the pack in place. The intention is that the weight of the pack should be carried by the supporting straps, not the tabs.

1908 WEB INFANTRY EQUIPMENT: 'MARCHING ORDER'

Information from: *The Pattern 1908 Web Infantry Equipment* (1913)
'Marching order' represented the full equipment of the First World War soldier on the march.

1 *Front view*

Fully loaded, the cartridge carriers contain 150 rounds of .303 ball ammunition. Each carrier has five pouches capable of carrying three chargers of five rounds each; each pouch is fastened by one of two studs, an upper and lower. In most cases, it is the upper stud that is used to fasten the pouch, to reduce unnecessary strain on the equipment. In 1914, the left-hand carriers were fitted with additional straps in order to prevent ammunition chargers falling out as men leaned against the trenches to fire. The set is adjusted to fit comfortably.

2 *Right view*

The pack is in position attached to the brace straps, the water bottle in its carrier suspended from the end of the brace straps (right) and the equivalent strap at the rear of the belt (left). The pack contains the greatcoat. According to the regulation arrangement, the entrenching tool carrier was also to be carried on this side; often it was carried to the rear of the soldier instead.

3 *Rear view*

The pack is fastened to the brace straps using two additional buckles that can be moved in position on the straps, and which are locked into place using equivalent tabs on the rear of the pack. To prevent the pack from bouncing up and down during marching, two supporting straps are provided, which buckle to the top of the pack and cross over it, passing through two loops to fasten, again with buckles, to two equivalent half-inch-width straps fixed to the rear of the cartridge carriers. Here the entrenching tool is carried at the rear (as was common), suspended from the brace straps; the haversack, bayonet and entrenching tool helve are carried on the left side of the soldier.

4 *Left view*

The haversack is worn over the bayonet and attached entrenching tool helve. The haversack contains the soldier's 'necessaries', rations etc; the helve is cleverly fixed to the bayonet by an additional web strap. The haversack is suspended from the brace strap ends, with the bayonet in its frog.

Field Service Pocket Book, 1914

A. Clothing	lb	oz
Boots, ankle, pair	4	0
Braces	0	4½
Cap, service dress with badge	0	9
Disc, identity, with cord	0	0¼
Drawers, woollen, pair	1	0½
Jacket, service dress and metal titles with field dressing	2	8
Knife, clasp, with marline spike and tin opener	0	8
Pay book (in right breast pocket of SD jacket)	0	2
Puttees, pair	0	13
Shirt	1	2
Socks, pair	0	4¼
Trousers, service dress	2	0½
Waistcoat, cardigan	1	7
Total (A)	**14**	**11**

A. Clothing (Highlanders)		
Apron, kilt	0	12⅞
Disc, identity, with cord	0	0¼
Drawers, woollen, pair	1	0½
Gaiters, Highland	0	10½
Garters and rosettes	0	2
Glengarry, with badge	0	9
Hosetops	0	4½
Jacket, service dress and metal titles with field dressing	2	8
Kilt	3	13
Knife, clasp, with marline spike and tin opener	0	8
Pay book (in right breast pocket of SD jacket)	0	2
Shirt	1	2
Shoes, Highland	3	8
Socks, pair	0	4¼
Trousers, service dress	2	0½
Waistcoat, cardigan	1	7
Total (A)	**18**	**3⅜**

B. Arms		
Rifle, with oil bottle, pull-through and sling	8	15¾
Bayonet and scabbard	1	8¾
Total (B)	**10**	**8½**

C. Ammunition		
Cartridges, S.A., ball, .303-inch, 150 rounds	9	0
Total (C)	**9**	**0**

D. Tools		
Implement, intrenching, pattern 1908		
Head	1	5¾
Helve	0	8¼
Carrier for ditto		
Head	0	9½
Helve	0	1¾
Total (D)	**9**	**0**

E. Accoutrements		
Water bottle, with carrier	1	6
Web equipment, pattern 1908		
Belt, waist	0	13
Braces, with buckle	0	11
Carriers, cartridge, 75 rounds		
Left	0	14½
Right	0	14½
Frog	0	3
Haversack, with	0	18¾
Knife	0	3
Fork	0	3
Spoon	0	2½
Pack, with supporting straps	1	11
Total (E)	**9**	**0**

F. Articles carried in the pack		
Cap, comforter	0	4
Holdall, containing	0	9¼
Laces	0	0¼
Toothbrush	0	0½
Razor and case	0	3
Shaving brush	0	1¼
Comb	0	1
Greatcoat, with metal titles	6	10¼
Housewife, fitted	0	3¼
Mess tin and cover	1	6½
Socks, worsted, pair	0	4¼
Soap, piece	0	3
Towel, hand	0	9
Total (F)	**10**	**1¾**

G. Rations and water		
Bread ration (unconsumed portion), say	0	12
Cheese	0	3
Iron ration		
Biscuit	0	12
Preserved meat (nominal)	1	0
Tea (⅜oz), sugar (2oz), salt (½oz), in a tin	0	6½
Cheese	0	3
Meat extract, 2 cubes	0	1
Water, 2 pints	2	8
Total (G)	**5**	**13½**

Total weight carried		
A. Clothing worn (non-Highlander)	14	11
A. Clothing worn (Highlander)	18	12⅜
B. Arms	10	8½
C. Ammunition	9	0
D. Tools	2	9¼
E. Accoutrements	8	4¼
F. Articles in pack	10	1¾
G. Rations and water	5	13½

Totals		
Normal weight carried by a non-highland private	61	0¼
Normal weight carried by a highland private	65	1⅜

(Added to this list in 1915–16 would be a steel helmet, and respirator.)

handicap of pulling up the belt and creating imbalance. Another advantage of the system was that it was directly fastened together, and could be removed as a whole; something that was lacking in the earlier 1903 set. With the opportunity to take the equipment off on the march – or simply to unbuckle it – meant that the 1908 equipment was easier to wear than the earlier set, especially as it did not have any straps crossing, and therefore constricting, the chest, a major drawback of the 1903 equipment set.

The fully assembled kit was known as 'marching order'. For each soldier thus equipped, he would be fully encumbered with all his equipment, field clothing and accoutrements, together with his rifle. Later in the war, the typical infantryman would also carry the respirator (in its appropriate haversack) and steel helmet. But soldiers would not usually be expected to carry this amount of equipment into the front line; packs would be left with the battalion transport lines and the kit would be transformed into 'battle order', the haversack worn on the shoulders in place of the pack.

The weight of the soldier's individual equipment varied through the war, but around 60lb was not unusual; indeed, it is not unusual today. An assessment of the weight was given in the officers' *Field Service Pocket Book, 1914*. Highland soldiers, with their distinctive dress and weighty woollen kilt, carried just that bit more than soldiers from England, Wales, Ireland or even the Scottish lowlands.

Though the 1908 webbing equipment set was supplied in waterproofed webbing, finished in a light khaki green colour, there was an inevitability that it would become dirty, even under normal conditions – let alone those encountered on the Western Front. Disassembling the equipment set was officially frowned upon, although it was essential if any form of cleaning was required. As such, the accompanying manual recommended that marks be made on the webbing set to indicate the optimum position of buckles and straps for each man, permitting easy reassembly. And with the possibility of confusion, every man was also expected to mark the inner sides of the equipment with his name and regimental number, in black ink.

The only officially sanctioned cleaning methods for the webbing set were the use of a clothes brush to remove dry mud, and simple washing, using warm water, soap and sponge, although a cleaner 'previously approved by the War Office' could also be applied. This cleaner was somewhat incongruously named 'blanco' – a composition supplied in cakes that was originally white, for the treatment of Victorian leather equipment, but that with the introduction of webbing was changed to shades of khaki. These shades varied, but during the First World War they were predominantly greenish, the two main types being 'Khaki-Blanco', with the greener-still shade 'Web-Blanco'. Although advertised as a cleaner, the blanco composition was actually designed to coat the webbing, thereby protecting it, and create a uniform colour. Supplied in zinc tins, blanco required water to activate it; either it was mixed into a slurry and added to the webbing, or it was worked as a powder into damp webbing. Either method required skill. As for the metalwork, the official manual of 1913, *The Pattern 1908 Web Infantry Equipment*, suggested that 'the metal work should not be polished but allowed to get dull, so as to avoid catching the rays of the sun'. This was certainly the case in the front line; out of it, brass was expected to gleam – and commercial equipment protectors were sold to ensure that the mutually incompatible mix of blanco and metal polish was kept separated.

Not all British soldiers were equipped with 1908 webbing, however. With the influx of a huge number of men into the armed forces at the beginning of the First World War, the Mills Equipment Company was seriously overstretched – it simply could not meet the demand placed upon it to supply regular, Territorial and service battalions with sufficient webbing equipment sets. As such, a stopgap was needed, one that would do the same job, but could be manufactured from leather – which, despite its many deficiencies, was freely available. The War Office commissioned a set of equipment in leather that was based upon the basic format of the webbing, but was quicker to make, and easier to source from overseas manufacturers.

As such, the 1914-pattern equipment was designed, based on the 1908 set. Officially

Information from: *The Pattern 1914 Leather Infantry Equipment* (1915)

Assembling the Pattern 1914 leather equipment.

The waist belt is adjusted at either end, so that it is tight, and the rear buckles and straps central to the rear of the belt, which is then laid out, inside downwards. The bayonet frog is then passed over the belt so that it will hang on the left hip, with the helve carrier strap buckled to it. The ammunition pouches are fixed to the belt by passing the two small straps on the back of the pouch around the belt, securing them tightly. The braces are then fastened to the rear buckles of the belt, the loose strap hanging one inch lower than the equivalent straps at the rear of the belt. At the front the braces are joined to the buckles at the top of the ammunition pouches, the straps passing behind them and matching the attached straps at the front of the carriers. The haversack is coupled to the left-hand side of the belt, connected to the two outer strap ends and fixed into position over the bayonet and helve. In normal circumstances, the entrenching tool carrier is secured to the right side, to the two inner strap ends. The water bottle carrier is then linked to the right side, using the two outer strap ends.

The pack is attached by laying the equipment face downwards and placing the pack upwards upon it. The straps without buckles on the belt are then passed through the buckles at the base of the pack, and tightly fastened, the remaining part of the strap running through the loops at

the base of the pack. The pack straps are then buckled to these and are passed diagonally across the pack to attach to the buckles at the top of the pack itself. Finally, the brace buckles are adjusted so that they line up with the securing tabs on the pack, which are then passed through the buckles to fix the pack in place. Unlike the 1908 equipment, which balanced the cartridge carriers with the pack, the straps provided with the 1914 threw the weight directly on to the belt, which was not ideal.

introduced on 30 August 1914, the official orders state that 'the equipment, except for the pack and haversack, is made of pliable hide leather, stained as near as possible to the colour of service dress'. Large orders were placed – but the first sets of this equipment were not available until months after the soldiers concerned had received their uniforms – not an ideal situation in a completely novice army.

Although using webbing for the haversack and large pack, the 1914-pattern equipment employed leather for waist belt, cross-straps, cartridge carriers (officially 'ammunition pouches'), entrenching tool holder, bayonet frog, water bottle cradle and entrenching tool carrier. Unlike the 1908 pattern, buckles were now equipped with tongues, this to prevent the leather slipping when wet. The belt, issued in 42- and 48-inch lengths, used a snake and hook fastener that was inherited from 19th-century belt patterns; a convenient hole in the leather backing to this fastener allowed the belt to be extended on the march for comfort. The 1914-pattern cartridge carriers were made as simple pouches, each designed to take two cotton bandoliers, each holding 50 cartridges in 5-round chargers. With an additional 10 rounds in a pocket, the pouches took 120 rounds in all, and therefore 30 rounds less than those of the 1908 equipment. The carriers were attached to the belt using small straps that fixed around it and buckled into position. Ungainly and unbalanced, these bulky leather pouches pulled down on the belt and were consequently uncomfortable to wear on the march.

The other components of the equipment set were similar in design to the webbing set, though the straps were narrower, with the braces tapering at the points of their attachment. As described in the official manual, *The Pattern 1914 Leather Infantry Equipment,* the essence of having the equipment well fitted was to ensure that the straps and buckles were as tight as possible; with front-line use, and with constant dampness, achieving this aim was often nigh-on impossible.

The 1914-pattern equipment set was serviceable, but less efficient at distributing weight than the original webbing, and was issued almost exclusively to service battalions. The sets were manufactured in the UK and

LEFT Soldier of the Buffs (Royal West Kent) equipped with Pattern 1914 leather equipment, Mark 1 helmet and SMLE rifle, 1918.

BELOW Pattern 1914 leather equipment, ammunition pouches and water bottle cradle.

Information from: *The Pattern 1914 Leather Infantry Equipment* (1915)

1 *Front view*

Fully loaded, the cartridge carriers contain 60 rounds of .303 ball ammunition. Each carrier has the capacity to take two cotton bandoliers, each bandolier comprising five cotton pouches with two chargers of five bullets in each. An internal pocket, designed to take two chargers of five bullets each, was also provided in each ammunition pouch. The pouches were interchangeable, neither with a dedicated 'side'.

2 *Right view*

The pack is in position attached to the brace straps, the water bottle in its carrier suspended from the end of the brace straps (right) and the equivalent strap at the rear of the belt (left). As with the 1908 pattern equipment, the pack contains the greatcoat. In this case, the steel helmet is held in position to the rear of the pack using the supporting straps.

3 *Rear view*

The pack, which is in webbing with leather straps, is attached to the brace straps using two additional tongued buckles, which are locked into position using leather tabs with holes that are to the rear of the pack. As with the 1908-pattern equipment, two supporting straps are provided to keep the pack from bouncing up and down while marching, but these are secured directly to the belt. As described above, the supporting straps were also used to carry the steel helmet – firmly held against the rear of the pack. The supporting straps fastened by tongued buckles directly to the belt. Here the leather entrenching tool holder is suspended from leather straps, and the haversack, similar in construction to the pack, is seen on the soldier's left side, over the bayonet and entrenching tool helve.

4 *Left view*

The haversack is worn over the bayonet and the entrenching tool helve. As with the webbing set, the helve was cleverly attached to the bayonet by an additional strap, in this case finished in leather. The haversack is suspended from the brace strap ends, with bayonet in its frog.

in the United States, with varying quality, and consisted of brown marbled leather, in some cases dyed green. In some battalions, the leather equipment was discarded in favour of webbing salvaged from the battlefield, or from field hospitals. In 1921, leather equipment was officially withdrawn from service and storage – with the result that few sets survive today.

Personal equipment and necessaries

Each soldier had to keep himself clean, tidy and presentable, even when in the trenches, and was issued with a set list of 'necessaries' under King's Regulations. Unless lucky enough to be a member of a rifle regiment – traditionally wearing black buttons and blackened insignia – brass fittings and insignia had to be burnished bright while out of the front line, and uniforms kept clean and in good repair. In the front line, of course, a more pragmatic approach had to be taken. It was expected that brass items should become dulled with exposure to the elements, as this would reduce the possibility of reflection off mirror-shined surfaces and, besides, the

troops had more than enough to do keeping body and soul together. Nevertheless, soldiers were expected to attend to their own personal cleanliness as far as was possible, shaving regularly – often in the dregs of tea left in a tin cup or mess tin – this at least an attempt to maintain morale.

Most of the soldier's necessaries were contained within a simple roll of cloth known as a 'holdall'. The holdall had a central strap of loops, their purpose to hold in position and carry all those items required for cleanliness in the field and the barracks. Typically the holdall contained: a cut-throat razor in its case, shaving brush, toothbrush and comb; button brass and spare bootlaces. In practice it also included the issue knife, fork and spoon, which were otherwise listed as separate necessaries to be carried in the pack. In accordance with clothing regulations, soldiers were expected to mark these small items of equipment, using a punch for metal objects (or an engraving tool), or ink for cloth, with their regimental number (or the last four digits) and their regiment or corps. For many young soldiers, shaving was a new experience, with downy cheeks requiring little more than a weekly shave. Army regulations insisted on a clean chin – and

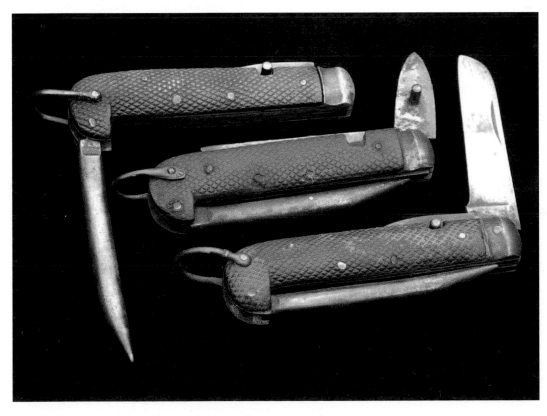

LEFT Examples of the soldier's clasp knife, showing the marline spike (top), tin opener (centre) and blade (bottom); the knife was usually carried on a cord around the waist.

The contents and manufacture of the holdall varied throughout the soldier's career. Composed of a canvas wrap with loops to secure the items of equipment in place, the material used changed during the war from a stiff canvas material to thin cotton. The issue of what the army called 'necessaries' was made on joining, and this was the soldier's 'free kit'. After this, it was up to the soldier to fill his holdall and keep it up to date, although 'no departure from the articles detailed in the lists' issued by the War Office was permitted. The holdall illustrated (from c1917–18) contains:

Spoon and fork: There are several different patterns known; these are typical. In the field, knives were probably discarded. Cutlery was stamped with the soldier's regimental number and battalion.

Toothbrush: The army put great store in maintaining oral health; without teeth,

BELOW The holdall and contents, c.1917.

soldiers would struggle to eat the food issued. Typical brushes had hard bristles set in bone handles, as in this example from 1918.

Razor: Cut-throat razors were issued in a card case and were marked to the soldier (with his number) and his battalion.

Shaving brush: Of many different patterns, soldiers had to replace them at their own expense.

Button brass: Essential to keep metal polish from staining the uniform, these were stamped with the regimental number and battalion.

Boot laces: Leather boot laces were used.

In this case, the soldier has supplemented his 'free kit' with other items: a 'trench art' letter opener made from scrap brass and spent cartridge; proprietary shaving soap; and a combination steel mirror and comb.

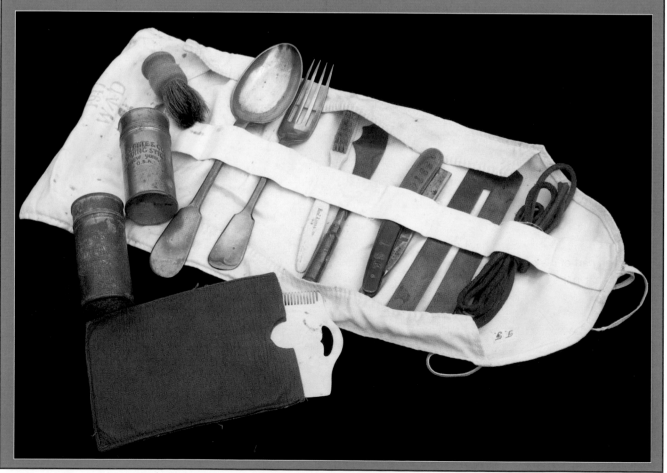

although the pre-war army had expected that soldiers would maintain a moustache, the upper lip was also kept cleanly shaven. The standard issue was a Sheffield-produced cut-throat razor, usually with horn fittings into which the soldier was once again expected to punch his regimental number and unit.

The roll provided a practical means of keeping objects together – although for the front-line soldier the essentials were more often than not carried in the most convenient position for use; there is evidence to suggest that the knife was discarded or lost (replaced by the clasp knife, which was an important issue item, most often worn around the waist on a cord), and that the spoon – with one side sharpened for general use – was carried tucked in the puttees.

The holdall also had a convenient pocket that provided the means of carrying additional items, perhaps including a shaving mirror, privately purchased, as well as soap, shaving requisites and the 'housewife'. The housewife – pronounced 'hussif' – was an essential piece of kit that held sewing materials: thread, needles, a thimble, wool, buttons and so on. The ravages of army life meant that some repair would be necessary and the 'housewife' provided a method of keeping the uniform in at least some semblance of order; by 1917–18, with the proliferation of badges and patches, it also allowed the soldier to add insignia to his tunic. The 'hussif' was simple in construction: a pocket of cotton material with a piece of serge for patching (and holding needles), closed by a flap.

Overseas, further equipment issues were required that would help support the soldier in the front line. The first of these were identification discs. Identity discs have not always been part of the soldier's traditional accoutrements in the British army, as identity in the field was originally provided by the 'Soldier's Service and Pay Book' (army form AB64), which was issued for overseas service, and carried in the right breast pocket of the service dress jacket. Clearly inadequate, this form of identification was supplemented by the addition of a single stamped aluminium disc, which carried the name, rank, serial number, unit details and religion (where appropriate). According to *Clothing Regulations, 1914*, the identity disc was only issued on mobilisation;

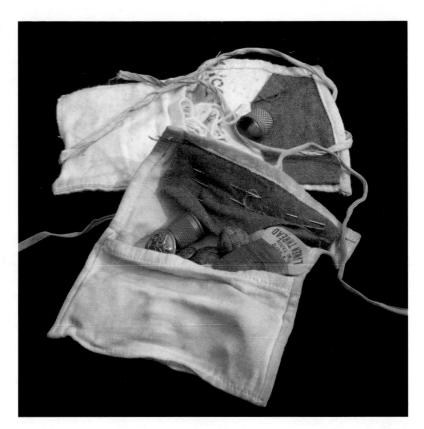

ABOVE The housewife – the soldier's sewing kit.

in preparation for the issue, though, discs were kept ready marked and the responsibility of the officer commanding. The issue of aluminium discs was short-lived, however, and this metal type was replaced by a red compressed-fibre version on the outbreak of war. Hardier than the pay book as a means of identification, there was, nonetheless, a problem with the disc system, as stipulated in *Field Service Regulations Part II,* 1909: 'Anyone concerned in burying a soldier, or finding a body after action, will remove the identity disc and paybook … and will note the number of the equipment and rifle, or anything else likely to assist in identification.' Once this single disc was removed from the body the chances of further identification were much reduced.

As such, in August 1916, a two-disc system was evolved, the discs themselves carrying the same information as before, in duplicate, but this time stamped on compressed vulcanised asbestos discs – a green octagonal one which, it was intended, would stay with the body, and a red disc that would be taken as part of the accounting procedure. Both were to be worn on a string around the neck – but as this often became dirty and clammy, soldiers were wont

IDENTITY DISCS

'Every officer and man will carry on a string around his neck an identity disc showing his name, number if any, unit and religion', *Field Service Regulations Part II, 1909*, (reprinted 1914).

1 *Aluminium disc:* The aluminium disc was introduced in August 1906, and was worn around the neck on a cord. It recorded the following information: name; regimental number; religion; regiment. This disc belonged to 202197 Corporal George E. Lewis of the 2/4 Somerset Light Infantry (religion: Church of England).

2 *Red fibre disc:* The vulcanised asbestos fibre disc superseded the aluminium disc in August 1914. This one was issued to Major R.C. Carr (religion: Church of England).

3 *Fibre disc pair:* Also made from vulcanised asbestos fibre, two discs were issued from August 1916. The intention was that while the green tag would remain with the body, the red one would be removed for recording purposes. This pair belonged to 241675 (formerly 4545) Private Edgar Retallick of the 2/5 King's Own Royal Lancaster Regiment (religion: Congregationalist Church).

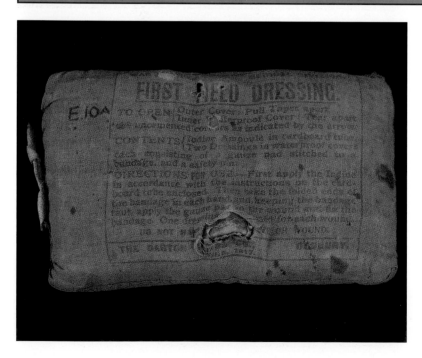

to carry the discs separately in the haversack or pack, or to rely on the commercially available metal versions that were produced at home and abroad. All were to be given the brutally frank name 'cold meat tickets' (resembling as they did the tags used in butchers' shops), as the war dragged on. And as was typical, local entrepreneurs soon adapted their trade to produce engraved or stamped versions for the troops in rear areas and base camps.

Field dressings were issued to all soldiers, to be kept in a pocket under the front flap of the service dress tunic, again specified in the *Field Service Regulations*. The first field dressing was intended for rudimentary first aid, and consisted of a packet containing two dressings – one for

LEFT First Field Dressing, 1917.

the entry wound, one for the exit (in the case of gunshot wounds). Early on, these pouches also contained safety pins and ampoules of iodine as a form of disinfectant to treat the wound; later in the war, after the value of the chemical having been questioned, it was left out of the set. In all cases, the idea was that a wounded man would have his own dressings used upon him; with so many injuries being caused by shellfire, larger dressings were needed than could be carried by an individual, and these special 'shell dressings' were carried by regimental stretcher-bearers in action.

In preparation for their first tour of the trenches, soldiers were also invited to make out their wills in advance of action. This was completed in that official record of their military service, the pay book. It was on page 13 of the AB64 that the proforma will was provided; soldiers moving up the line for the first time were to complete this. Pre-war, the soldier was issued with a linen-covered peacetime 'Small Book'; this was supplemented with the issue of the AB64, 'Soldier's Service and Pay Book', given to every soldier going on active service. The pay book served as a logbook of service, but also included personal and family details (including next of kin), regimental number, dates of enlistment, ranks and awards attained, skill at arms, charges, a sick record, and a record of pay issued. The pay book acted as a

ABOVE The First Field Dressing was carried in a pocket inside the jacket.

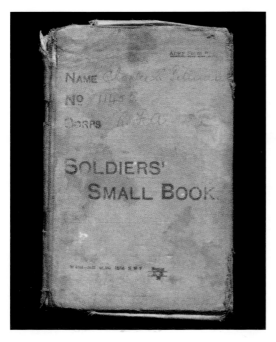

LEFT Soldier's Small Book (left) and Pay Book (right).

ABOVE **The Pay Book was carried in the right breast pocket for easy access.**

BELOW **Bully beef tin and cloth bag for the 'unexpired portion' of the soldier's rations.**

'passport'; a document that was to be carried at all times and to be produced on request for examination by officers or regimental/military police. This slim, brown pocket book was a valuable document, proof of identification of the soldier, both as a battlefield casualty and when receiving pay.

Another issue essential for all soldiers 'going up the line' was the provision of 'iron rations', food to be carried in action and intended to provide sustenance only under the direst of circumstances. Iron rations comprised a tin of 'bully beef', some biscuits, and a tin containing tea and sugar. It was a 'crime' to dip into these rations unless the order was given to do so from an officer, and were to be used only in an emergency. Carried in the haversack, or sometimes in a small cloth bag (intended for the 'unexpired' portion of a day's ration) attached to the belt or equipment, these would be carried into action, along with a full water bottle. The accompanying army biscuits were so hard that men had to have reasonable teeth – a requirement of the medical inspection on enlistment – to bite into them, or they had to be ground into a powder and mixed with water to make rudimentary desserts or to bulk up food in the front line.

Training the soldier

The strains that had been felt by the army in supplying the influx of new men with uniforms and equipment were magnified when it came to housing the new recruits. With the Haldane reforms of the army in 1908 came a focus on a regimental depot located regionally in order to act as a centre for recruitment. Regiments that proudly carried the name of their county usually had a depot and barracks located within a prominent county town. It was from here that the two regular battalions found in most regiments served in turn during peacetime, as well as replacing each other overseas in order to take on Imperial duties, garrisoning the outposts of the Empire. Also in peacetime it was the base, in most cases, to the third, Special Reserve, battalion, which acted as a 'home' to the recruits before they were posted to the regular battalions. These

men would be housed in the regimental barracks, often located in old buildings: purpose-built, if austere, before going on to their normal postings.

For the part-time Territorials, 'home' would be one of the many drill halls scattered about the country, and it would be here that soldiers would parade on Saturday afternoons – earning them the nickname 'Saturday night soldiers'. With the only obligation to house these men being an annual two-week camp for training, accommodation was usually less of an issue, and was usually in hutted or tented camps across Britain during the summer – when the weather was more forgiving to this type of lodging. With the coming of war, and the creation of a mass citizen army, a major problem was the billeting of large numbers of new recruits. The response was to build hutted encampments; but even these would require considerable investment of time. In the meantime, while the new camps were being built, tented accommodation was provided – adequate for

a two-week Territorial field camp, but hardly the perfect setting to train an amateur army to the peak of military effectiveness. By mid-1915, most of the tented quarters had been replaced by wooden huts, and conditions improved. Postcards sent from the camp set out to outline its regularity for the people back home, like this one, from early 1915:

6.30	Reveille
6.45	Rouse Parade
7.00	Breakfast
8.15	Company Officer's Parade
8.45	Manoeuvres
11.15	Swedish Drill
1.00	Dinner
2.15	Rifle Drill
3.15	Lecture by Officer
4.30	Dismiss
5.00	Tea
6.00	Free time
10.00	Last Post
10.15	Lights out
10.30	Inspection of Guards

ABOVE Territorial soldiers at a training camp, c.1914. Territorials, part-time soldiers, were committed to a two-week training camp every year.

With the men settled in their camps, the main job of the army instructors was to create a fit, efficient fighting force attuned to discipline and steady under fire, and took training seriously. As stated in the textbook *Infantry Training, 1914*: 'The object to be aimed at in the training of the infantry soldier is to make him, mentally and physically, a better man than his adversary on the field of battle.' *Infantry Training* also set out the instruction course syllabus that would see the transition of the recruit to trained soldier. There were eleven components to this: 1. the development of a soldierly spirit; 2. instruction in barrack and camp duties; 3. physical training; 4. infantry training; 5. marching and running; 6. musketry instruction; 7. movements at night; 8. guards and outposts; 9. duties of soldier in the field; 10. use of entrenching equipment; and 11. bayonet fighting. The average recruit might expect to receive training in all of these on his journey to becoming a soldier.

The army was clear, even in wartime, that the development of 'soldierly spirit' was a vital part of training. Although there was pressure to fill the ranks, according to *Drill and Field Training* (1914), 'good character' was still an essential condition of enlistment in the British army. In 1914, the essence of this character and of soldierly spirit was boiled down to the statement: 'The ideal which inspires a man is that of willing self-sacrifice for the welfare of the State and the good of his fellow-citizens. To this ideal, should occasion arise, the soldier must be faithful unto death.' These high ideals were to be further developed, it was hoped, by means of training, and particularly through the development of discipline and initiative; and via ceremonial parades, inspections and pride in the regiment. This diet of training included a wide range of drill designed to create the basis of a 'soldierly spirit'.

Discipline also extended to inspection of kit, the nature and cleanliness of the recruit's barracks, and his personal appearance and hygiene – particularly seen in the attention to detail in the care of the recruit's feet. With physical exercise and route marching at the top of the list in developing the body and the soldierly spirit, the concentration on feet is understandable. It would become even more important once men moved to France and were made to trek long distances on hard roads, before going into the trenches and suffering their immersion in the cold water and mud that invested most of the ditches used as the firing line in France and Flanders. Feet were regularly inspected; socks changed and greased to prevent blistering on long tramps; feet dusted with a concoction of boracic acid, talc and salicylic acid after drying. Such niceties would be difficult on the march, however.

According to the *Manual of Military Hygiene 1912* (reprinted 1914), marching was an essential part of a soldier's training: 'The chief work of the infantry soldier is marching. …In preparing for a campaign or series of marches, care must be taken that only fit men form part of the columns.' Learning how to march was important in the physical development of the average soldier. Gymnastics, Swedish drill, competitive sports and running formed a large segment of the remainder of the army's drive to develop the recruit into a fighting man. In the army's *Manual of Physical Training, 1908* (reprinted with amendments 1914), 'the object of physical training is the production of a state of health and general physical fitness in order that the body may be enabled to withstand the strains of daily life and to perform the work required of it without injury to the system'.

THE NECESSARY STANDARD OF EFFICIENCY EXPECTED FROM A RECRUIT, 1914

From: *Infantry Training (4-Company Organisation), 1914*

A The recruit must be able to turn out correctly in marching order and fit to take his place in the ranks of his company in close and extended order drill.

B Carry out an ordinary route march in marching order.

C Have completed his recruit gymnastic training.

D Be sufficiently trained in musketry and visual training to commence a recruit's course of musketry immediately after being dismissed recruit training.

E Be sufficiently trained to take part in night operations.

F Understand the principles of protection and his duties on guard or outpost.

G Be able to use his entrenching tools and understand the method of carrying tools.

H Be well grounded in bayonet fighting.

With large numbers of civilians coming into the army, training involved a simple diet of physical training, involving the application of the Swedish drill system of 'physical jerks' – military-style gymnastics invented by Pehr Henrik Ling in the late 19th century. Described in detail in the *Manual of Physical Training*, each recruit was put on a path to fitness by progression through tables of development in order that he could meet a set of simple requirements: 'A soldier should be well disciplined, a good marcher, intelligent, smart, active and quick, able to surmount obstacles in the field and capable of withstanding all the strains and hardships of active service.'

In order to attain these ideals, alongside fitness the army was keen to inculcate discipline and precision in drill, and this formed a major part of the training of new recruits. *Infantry Training (4-Company Organisation), 1914* was the standard drill and training 'bible' for the British army from the outbreak of war. A compact book designed to be carried in the pocket, its pages featured all the wisdom

ABOVE Recruits performing 'physical jerks' in 1915. In the background can be seen a frame for bayonet practice.

LEFT A Drill Sergeant, with pace stick, casts a critical eye over his recruits.

From: *Infantry Training (4-Company Organisation), 1914*

Squad-Attention: On the order, the squad springs up to a position with the heels together and in line, the feet turned out at an angle of 45 degrees, and the knees held straight. The body should be erect and carried evenly over the thighs, with the shoulders down and moderately back, thereby bringing the chest into its natural position without straining.

The arms should be hanging easily from the shoulders, though with the thumbs immediately behind the seams of the trousers, palms towards the thighs, partially closed. The neck should be erect, the head balanced evenly upon it, and not poked forwards. The idea is a position of readiness, but with no stiffness and straining. From the position of attention, soldiers will take the 'At Ease' position when ordered to do so.

required to ensure that soldiers were capable of acting as one and with precision when so ordered. A new soldier had to learn how to operate in many different units available to him, from battalions to squads. Working in small numbers for practice, recruits would be trained in the rudiments of military drill, with and without arms. Squad drill without arms introduced the basics: standing at ease and to attention, saluting and marching at different rates. Soldiers were taught to heed the sergeant major's pace stick, and to drill to the accompaniment of a drum in

the first instance. As prescribed by the army, the length of pace in slow and quick time was 30in, double time 40in. This would be measured using the sergeant major's stick to ensure consistency. At marching distances of 100–200yds on the drill ground, squads would be put through their paces: 120 paces (or 100yds) a minute in quick time; or 140 paces when not encumbered by infantry 'Marching Order' equipment. Learning the positions of 'at ease', and 'at attention' were also important, as was the correct means of saluting, both to the front, and to the side.

1–3 *Saluting to the front.*
Standing to attention, the right hand is brought smartly up, with a circular motion, to the head. The palm is to the front, the fingers extended and close together, the point of the forefinger one inch above the right eye, or touching the peak of the cap just below the right eyebrow, thumb close to the forefinger, elbow in line, nearly square with the shoulder. Then the arm is cut away smartly to the side.

4–6 *Saluting to the side*
Saluting to the side is carried out on the command right- (or left-) hand salute. It is carried out as with saluting to the front, with the exception that as the hand is brought up to the salute, the head is turned towards the person receiving the salute. The salute is made with the hand furthest from the person saluted.

Saluting was a significant component of drill, and had to be carried out with precision in order to pay compliment to the officer being saluted. Soldiers were trained to salute officers on the third pace before reaching him, lowering the hand on the third pace after reaching him. There were other regulations, too; if sitting, the soldier must come to attention first; if carrying a cane or swagger stick, this was to be tucked under the 'disengaged arm'; and if the soldier was missing his cap, he was simply to come to attention, or turn his head smartly in the direction of his superior. The regulations

for saluting covered several pages of *Infantry Training.*

Learning how to execute drill without carrying arms was one thing; doing it while handling the SMLE rifle was quite another. Saluting an officer while carrying a rifle was also learned.

For the average soldier, military instruction included proper care and use of his principal weapon, the Rifle, Short, Magazine Lee-Enfield (SMLE) rifle: according to the *Musketry Regulations, Part I, 1909* (reprinted 1914), 'Musketry training is to render the individual soldier proficient in the use of small arms, to

SEQUENCE: SQUAD DRILL WITH ARMS

From: *Infantry Training (4-Company Organisation), 1914*

Arms at the order

The rifle is held perpendicular to the side, with its butt on the ground, and its toe in line with the toe of the right foot. The right arm should be holding the rifle at or near the band, back of the hand to the right, thumb against the thigh. **[1]**

Slope arms from the order

1. The rifle is lifted upwards with the right hand, the soldier catching it with his left hand at the back-sight and his right hand at the small of the butt, thumb to the left, elbow to the rear. **[2]**

2. Carrying the rifle across the body, the rifle is placed flat on the shoulder, the magazine kept outwards from the body. The butt is seized with the left hand. The soldier's left arm should have its upper part held vertically, the lower part horizontally, and the heel of the butt should be in line with the centre of the right thigh. **[3]**

3. The right arm is now moved from the rifle and 'cut away' smartly to the side. **[4]**

Present arms from the slope

1. The rifle is seized at the small (between the butt and the trigger guard), with both arms kept close to the body. **[5]**

2. The rifle is raised with the right hands so that it is perpendicular in front of the body, with the sling to the left; at the same time the left hand is placed smartly upon the stock, with the wrist on the magazine, the point of the thumb in line with the soldier's mouth. The soldier's left elbow is to be kept close to the butt, while his right elbow and the butt should be kept close to the body. **[6]**

3. The rifle is then brought down perpendicularly, so that it is in front of the centre of the body with its guard to the front. The rifle is held lightly at the full extent of the right arm, with the soldier's fingers slanting downwards, while the left hand is brought up to meet the rifle smartly, immediately behind the back-sight, with the soldier's thumb pointing towards the muzzle. The weight of the rifle is supported by the left hand. While carrying out this manoeuvre, the hollow of the right foot is brought against the heel of the left foot, with both knees held straight. **[7]**

Order from the slope

1. The rifle is brought down to the full extent of the left arm, with the right hand meeting it between the back-sight and the band, with the right arm kept close to the body. **[8]**
2. The rifle is then brought to the right side, with the left hand grasping the nose cap, and the butt just clear of the ground. **[9]**
3. The butt is then placed quietly on the ground, and the left hand is 'cut away' to the left side. **[10]**

Stand at ease from the order

Keeping the legs straight, the soldier carries his left foot about 12 inches further to the left, so that the weight of the body rests equally on both feet. The muzzle of the rifle is inclined slightly to the front with the soldier's right hand, his right arm close to his side, while his left arm is kept in position.

From: *Infantry Training (4-Company Organisation), 1914*

1 When a soldier, other than a rifleman, carrying a rifle passes or addresses an officer he will do so at the slope, and will salute by carrying the right hand smartly to the small of the butt, the forearm held horizontal, the back of the hand to the front, fingers straight. If passing an officer, the soldier will salute on the third pace before reaching him, and will cut away the right hand on the third pace after passing him.

2 In passing an officer the soldier will always turn his head towards him.

3 If halted when an officer passes, the soldier will turn his head towards him and stand at the order.

make him acquainted with the capabilities of the weapon with which he is armed, and to give him confidence in its power and accuracy.' But in Kitchener's New Army, valuable weapons such as the SMLE would be in short supply, and trainees would have to make do with wooden stand-ins, or imports from Canada or Japan while learning how to carry out manoeuvres with appropriate military bearing. The use of the bayonet was also deemed essential, and bayonet fighting would always be high on the training agenda. Preparation to go overseas required the completion of instruction, and the obligatory course of musketry, using both the SMLE and a smaller-bore .22 rifle for target shooting. Yet 'skill at arms' training would not necessarily translate into action in the field.

The Rifle, Short, Magazine Lee-Enfield (SMLE)

The principal weapon of the British soldier from 1904 was the Short, Magazine Lee-Enfield rifle, SMLE to most soldiers. The SMLE was based on its predecessor, the Magazine, Lee-Enfield (MLE), first introduced in 1895. The MLE was the first British service rifle to equipped with a ten-round magazine, and was famed for its bolt action, which cocked the striker when the bolt was closed, a swift action, important in battle, meaning the weapon could be cocked and fired rapidly.

The intention was to build on the reliability of

this arm, but to shorten it, lighten it, and provide the means of its loading through a charger-fed magazine system – thereby capitalising on its superior bolt action. The SMLE Mark I was developed following experiences with the MLE in the Boer War, which indicated that a lighter, more easily handled, better sighting and quicker loading weapon was needed. The resulting rifle, the SMLE, was to appear on 23 December 1902. It was 5in shorter than its forerunner (although with three butt sizes fitted to soldiers of differing stature), and was both easier to handle and capable of being used as an infantry rifle and a cavalry carbine.

The charger system used by the SMLE allowed for five rounds to be loaded at a time, the magazine holding ten all together. In British service, the 'charger' was a clip that held five rounds of the standard Mark VII cartridges – known as the 'ball cartridge'. The charger was discarded when the cartridges were pressed home, forced downwards into the spring-loaded magazine that was capable of holding ten rounds in total. The high-capacity magazine and efficient bolt action meant that in the right hands the rifle had an impressive rate of fire. Well-trained soldiers could fire around 15 aimed bullets a minute with the SMLE – while the record, set in 1914, was 38 bullets fired in a minute, a prodigious rate of fire.

The SMLE was to undergo several modifications through to its last model, the Mark VI, in 1926. It would be one of the most admired bolt-action rifles in history. The early Mark I rifles had the provision for a long-range volley sight – inaccurate, but capable in the right hands of putting down a volley with an effective range of 1,500–2,000yds. The SMLE Mark III, introduced in January 1907 with changes to its sights and charger loading system, was the main rifle to be used during the war; from January 1916 simplifications to this rifle (SMLE Mark III*) were made in order to speed up production for the New Army. Among other things, the volley sights, no longer needed in trench warfare with the decline in musketry skills, were omitted, along with such niceties as the magazine cut-off.

RIGHT The breech, showing magazine cut off and charger guide.

THE RIFLE, SHORT, MAGAZINE LEE-ENFIELD MARK III

From: *Musketry Regulations Part I, 1909* (reprinted with amendments 1914)

Specifications

Weight of rifle with magazine empty, Mark III	8lb 10½oz
Weight of sword bayonet without scabbard	1lb 0½oz
Length of butt, long	1ft 1 13/16 in
Length of butt, normal	1ft 1 5/16 in
Length of butt, short*	1ft 0 13/16 in
Length of rifle, with normal length of butt, without sword bayonet*	3ft 8½in
Length of rifle, with normal length of butt, with sword bayonet*	5ft 2in
Length of barrel	2ft 1¼in
Calibre	.303in
Rifling system	Enfield
Twist of rifling	left hand; 1 turn in 10in, or 33 calibres
Muzzle velocity	Mark VII ammunition, 2,440ft/s
Number of grooves	5
Depth of grooves at muzzle	.0065in
Depth of grooves at breech, to within 14in of muzzle	.00575in
Width of lands	.0936in
Sighting system	Adjustable blade fore-sight, radial back-sight, with vertical adjustment and windgauge
Method of loading	Charger, holding five cartridges

*Fitted to each man, individually.

Names of the parts of Rifle, Short MLE, Mark III

From: *Musketry Regulations Part I, 1909* (reprinted with amendments 1914)

1. Blade fore-sight.
2. Fore-sight block.
3. Band fore-sight block.
4. Key fore-sight block.
5. Crosspin fore-sight block.
5A. Back-sight bed.
6. Back-sight bed crosspin.
6A. Back-sight bed sight spring screw.
7. Back-sight leaf.
8. Back-sight slide.
9. Back-sight slide catch.
10. Back-sight fine adjustment worm wheel.
10A. Windgauge.
10B. Windgauge screw.
11. Back-sight ramps.
12. Seating for safety catch.
13. Safety catch.
14. Locking bolt system.
15. Bolt.
16. Bolt head.
17. Striker.
18. Cocking-piece.
19. Striker collar with stud.

20. Bolt-head tenon.
22. Cocking-piece locking recesses.
23. Locking bolt.
24. Locking bolt flat.
25. Locking bolt thumb-piece.
26. Locking bolt aperture sight stem.
27. Locking bolt stop pin recesses.
28. Locking bolt safety catch stem.
29. Locking bolt safety catch arm.
30. Locking bolt screw threads.
31. Locking bolt seating .
32. Bolt arm grooves.
33. Sear.
34. Sear seating.
35. Sear spring.
36. Magazine catch.
37. Full bent of cocking-piece.
38. Short arm of sear.
39. Trigger rib.
40. Trigger rib.
41. Trigger.
42. Trigger axis pin.
41A. Magazine case.
41B. Magazine platform spring.

41C. Magazine auxiliary spring.
43. Guard trigger.
44. Stock fore-end.
45. Spring and stud fore-end.
46. Protector back-sight.
47. Handguard front and rear.
48. Spring handguard rear.
49. Lower band groove.
50. Lower band.
51. Nosecap.
52. Protector fore-sight.
53. Sword bar.
54. Boss for ring of sword bayonet crosspiece.
55. Swivel seating.
56. Swivel piling.
57. Nosecap barrel opening.
58. Inner band.
59. Inner band screw.
60. Inner band screw spring.
61. Butt sling swivel.
62. Sword bayonet, pattern '07
64. Bridge charger guide.
65. Cut-off.

PLATE II.
SHORT RIFLE, MAGAZINE LEE-ENFIELD (MARK III).

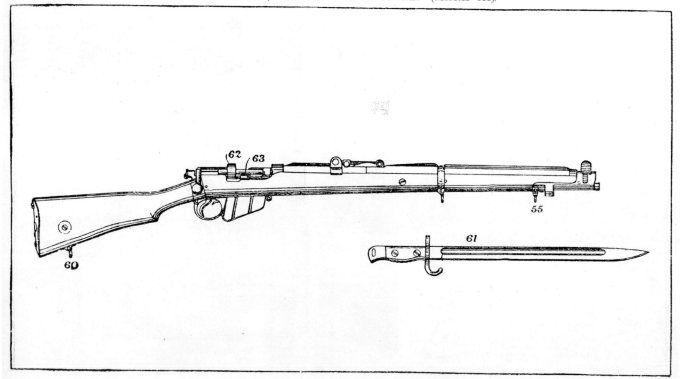

PLATE III.
SHORT RIFLE, MAGAZINE LEE-ENFIELD (MARK III).

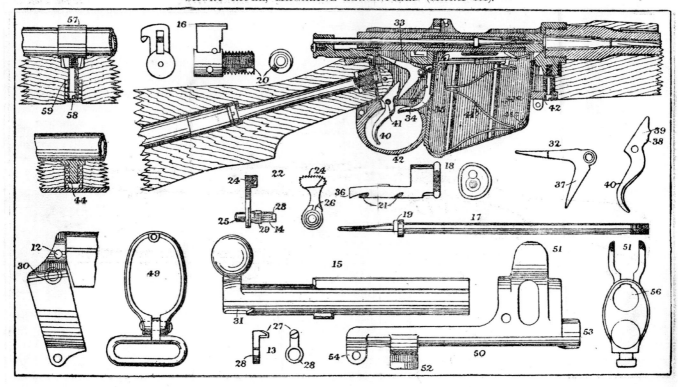

PLATE IV.
SHORT RIFLE, MAGAZINE LEE-ENFIELD (MARK III).

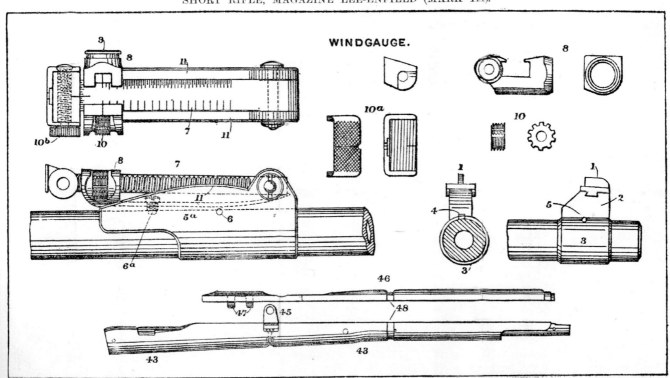

WINDGAUGE.

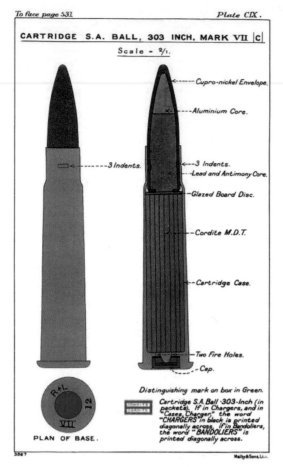

RIGHT The Mk VII bullet.

BELOW Charger of five Mark VII bullets, recovered from a dugout in the Ypres Salient.

To face page 531.   *Plate CIX.*

CARTRIDGE S.A. BALL, 303 INCH, MARK VII |C|

Scale - 2/1.

Cupro-nickel Envelope.
Aluminium Core.
3 Indents.
3 Indents.
Lead and Antimony Core.
Glazed Board Disc.
Cordite M.D.T.
Cartridge Case.
Two Fire Holes.
Cap.

R↑L
12
VII
PLAN OF BASE.

Distinguishing mark on box in Green.

Cartridge S.A. Ball ·303-Inch (in packets). If in Chargers, and in "Cases, Chargers" the word "CHARGERS" in black is printed diagonally across, if in Bandoliers, the word "BANDOLIERS" is printed diagonally across.

The SMLE was loaded with the Mark VII bullet, which replaced the Mark VI in military service in 1904 and is distinguished from the earlier cartridge by its pointed, rather than rounded, bullet shape. The Mark VII bullet, also used in the Vickers and Lewis machine guns, was coated in cupro-nickel and had a core of lead and antimony, with an aluminium tip – making it stable but tail heavy in flight. The bullet was propelled by cordite and left the rifle with a muzzle velocity of 2,440ft/s. Cartridges were supplied in five-pocket cotton bandoliers or in boxes that were readily accessible to all soldiers during their tours of the trenches; it is not surprising that unfired Mark VII cartridges are common in archaeological digs.

All soldiers had to be proficient in arms drill, and competent in handling and cleaning their arms. A worn rifle meant inaccuracy and a liability; according to *Musketry Regulations Part I, 1909*, with care a rifle could be expected to fire at least 5,000 rounds before it became unserviceable. Wear of the rifle was primarily due to friction as the bullet passed through; to the heat generated when this happened; and finally through the overuse of the gauze supplied with the pull-through when cleaning the bore. To arrest this wear soldiers were expected to clean their rifles regularly, and especially after firing, in order to control the amount of residue that could easily become welded to the interior of the bore. The SMLE was provided with a cleaning kit held within the butt, and accessed through the butt trap. This consisted of a brass oil bottle, which unscrewed to reveal a spoon that could be used to ladle machine oil ('Russian petroleum') into the component parts; and a brass-weighted cord 'pull-through' that was used to drag oiled flannelette cloth through the bore to clean it, or, when used with the gauze, to physically scour residue left by firing the rifle. Regulations stipulated that this kit should be kept in the butt of the rifle, not separately within the haversack.

The purpose of cleaning the rifle was to remove 'fouling' left by its use, caused both by the action of gasses and the solids of combustion. Removal of residues required the recruit to understand the value and importance of using the pull-through, flannelette strips and oil bottle. Under ideal

CLEANING THE RIFLE

From: *Musketry Regulations Part I, 1909* (reprinted with amendments 1914)

1 *Removing the bolt*
The bolt is removed by raising the knob as far as it will go, drawing back the bolthead to the resisting shoulder, and then pushing it up to release the spring. Moving the bolthead to the left, the bolt can then be removed completely. The bolt is replaced after cleaning.

2 *Cleaning the exterior of the action*
The action to be cleaned daily by the simple expedient of applying an oily rag.

3 *Cleaning the bore*
The bore to be kept oiled until it is ready to fire; the oil is to be removed before firing, as the presence of lubricant increases thrust on the bolthead. Removal of the oil carried out by the use of the pull-through and a piece of dry flannelette.

4 *Using the pull-through*
After firing, it is essential to clean the bore as soon as possible, and especially while it is still warm. Five or six pints of boiling water poured through the barrel, using a funnel at the breech, are valuable in removing fouling. In the absence of boiling water, the bore is cleaned by the use of the pull-through. Removing the bolt, the brass weight is dropped through the bore from the breech to the muzzle. If necessary, severe fouling is removed by the use of the gauze, clamped to the string of the pull-through. Abrasive, the gauze is loaded with oil to reduce wear. Having pulled the string through several times, a piece of oil-impregnated flannelette is then pulled through the bore to relubricate it.

57

DRILL, RIFLE INSPECTION

From: *Infantry Training (4-Company Organisation), 1909* (reprinted with amendments 1914)

Usually carried out in a squad, the men to be inspected took a pace forward for their weapons to be inspected. NCOs carried

a device to enable this, a clever magnifier that would allow the detection of even the smallest amount of fouling in the barrel.

RIGHT The butt trap; here the oil bottle and pull-through was stored.

conditions the rifle barrel would be treated with boiling water, carefully poured into the barrel, avoiding the action at all costs. The use of boiling water would prevent the build up of residue, as well as the capacity of the barrel to rust under extreme conditions.

With the rifle considered to be the 'soldier's best friend', great store was placed upon training the soldier to maintain his weapon. Inspections were regular, and meticulous. They would not only ensure that the soldier was looking after his arms, but would also allow officers and NCOs to identify any problems that could be referred to the armourer for rectification, thereby arresting any problems before a soldier went overseas and was required to use his rifle in action.

In Kitchener's New Army, valuable weapons such as the SMLE were in short supply, and trainees would have to make do with wooden stand-ins while learning how to carry out manoeuvres with appropriate military bearing. In August 1914, the whole stock of serviceable

For inspection, port arms

1 Lift the rifle with the right hand across the body, its guard to the left and downwards, the rifle crossing the right shoulder, and with the left hand close behind the back-sight, thumb and fingers round the rifle, both elbows close to the body. **[1]**

2 Turn the safety catch over, and pull out the cut-off. Seizing the knob with the thumb and forefinger, the bolt is drawn back to its fullest extent, the butt is then grasped with the right hand immediately behind the bolt, the thumb pointing towards the muzzle. **[2,3]**

Ease springs

From the position above, the bolt is worked rapidly backwards and forwards until all cartridges are removed, allowing them to fall to the ground. Pressing the trigger, the cut-off is then closed, and the safety catch is turned over, the hand returning to the small of the rifle.

Order arms

1 Holding the rifle firmly in the left hand, it is seized with the right hand at the band. **[4]**

2 The rifle is brought to the right side, seizing it with the left hand around the nose cap, butt just clear of the ground.

3 The butt is then placed quietly upon the ground, the left hand is then cut away to the side. **[5]**

rifles stood at a little less than 800,000, and just over half of these were the SMLE; with most of these weapons already issued, there was a reserve of no more than 10%. With the two main manufacturers (the Royal Small Arms Factory, Enfield (RSA) and the Birmingham Small Arms Company (BSA)) already committed, the War Office brought in two other companies to supply the SMLE (Vickers and the Standard Small Arms Company), and filled the gap with rifles from other countries. Ross rifles from Canada and Japanese Arisaka rifles were used in training by Kitchener's Army men, alongside the obsolete long Lee-Enfield.

The War Office manual *Musketry Regulations Part I, 1909* (reprinted with amendments 1914) defined the basis for rifle training with the SMLE: 'To render the individual soldier proficient in the use of small arms, to make him acquainted with the capabilities of the weapon with which he is armed, and to give him confidence in its power and accuracy.' Accompanied by lectures on the theory of rifle firing, the recruit was taken

LEFT Soldier of the Queen's (Royal West Surrey) Regiment equipped with Long Lee and 1888 pattern bayonet.

FIRING WHILE STANDING

From: *Musketry Regulations Part I, 1909* (reprinted with amendments 1914)

The standing position 'will as a rule be used on service to fire from breastworks, high walls, and cover … or to take a snap shot when advancing'. In the trenches, it was adopted while firing from the fire step.

To load **[1,2]**
On the command 'Load', turn half right, carrying the left foot to the left and slightly forward so the body is equally balanced on both feet. Bring the rifle to the right side in front of the hip, with the muzzle pointing upwards, small of the butt just in front of the hip, grasping the stock with the left hand immediately in front of the magazine. Turn the safety catch completely over to the front with the thumb or forefinger. Pull out the cut-off, pressing it downwards with the thumb, then seize the knob with the forefinger and thumb of the right hand, turn it sharply upwards, drawing back the bolt to the fullest extent. Taking a charger between the thumb and first two fingers of the right hand, place it vertically between the guides. Then, placing the ball of the thumb

immediately in front of the charger, and hooking the forefinger under the cut-off, force the cartridges down with a firm pressure until the top cartridge has engaged with the magazine. (Though the magazine will take two charges of five cartridges, it is more usual to load only one.) Forcing the bolt sharply home, turning the knob well down, turn the safety catch over to the rear.

To aim and fire **[3,4]**
After loading, direct eyes on the mark. Bring the rifle into the hollow of the right shoulder, press it in with the left hand, grasping the small with the thumb and three fingers of the right hand, place the forefinger round the lower part of the trigger, and exert sufficient pressure to take the first pull, the back-sight to be upright, the left elbow well under the rifle, right elbow a little lower than the right shoulder; as the rifle touches the shoulder bring the cheek down to the butt, keeping the face well back from the right hand and cocking piece, close the left eye, align the sights in the mark, restrain the breathing, and press the trigger.

FIRING WHILE PRONE

From: Musketry Regulations Part I, 1909 (reprinted with amendments 1914)

The prone position 'will generally be adopted by troops on open ground, or when firing from continuous low cover, or from behind small rocks, etc'. Recruits were 'trained to assume the prone position rapidly' and to 'perform the loading and aiming motions with as little movement as possible', in order to take full advantage of their position on open ground.

To lie down [1]
Turn half right, bring the rifle to the right side (as when standing). Place the right hand on the ground, and lie down on the stomach obliquely to the line of fire, with legs separated, left shoulder well forward, left arm extended to the front, rifle rested on the ground in a convenient position, muzzle pointing to the front.

To load [2]
Maintaining the prone position, carry out the loading procedure used while standing.

To aim and fire [3]
Maintaining the prone position, carry out the aiming and firing procedure used while standing.

61

FIRING WHILE KNEELING

From: *Musketry Regulations Part I, 1909* (reprinted with amendments 1914)

The kneeling position was to be used 'mainly when firing from continuous cover, such as a low wall, bank or hedge …'.

Kneeling **[1]**
The soldier can kneel on either or both knees. When using a single knee, the body is supported on the heel if comfortable, the left knee will be in advance of the left heel, the left elbow resting on or over the left knee. The left leg, hand and arm, and the right shoulder, should be in the same vertical plane.

To load **[2]**
Maintaining the kneeling position, carry out the loading procedure used while standing.

To aim and fire **[3]**
Maintaining the kneeling position, carry out the aiming and firing procedure used while standing.

through his paces to learn the fundamentals before progressing to actually firing his weapon. Aiming practice – learning how to line the back- and fore-sights accurately – was first, before progressing to firing practice. Arranged in groups of seven men, the instructor first explained the finer points of trigger-pressing before proceeding to actually shooting the weapon. Essential was the need to gain the correct stance when firing standing, kneeling or prone. The positions for firing and loading while standing, lying prone and kneeling (plus other positions) were defined in *Musketry Regulations Part I, 1909* and recruits were instructed in their use and advantages.

While the standing position was the one most adopted during a soldier's spell 'in the trenches', it was the prone and kneeling positions, from behind whatever cover could be found, that would be used in the much-anticipated return to open warfare.

Knowing how to fire and load while kneeling was also important, especially when firing from hedgerows or destroyed buildings.

In all cases, recruits were instructed in the value of cover, as well as the need to, in soldiers' parlance, 'keep their nappers down'. Exaggerated movements were also discouraged as they tended to attract attention. All new soldiers were taught the need to aim and fire steadily in all positions and from all types of cover, and were encouraged to combine a rapidity of loading with that of aiming and firing accurately. For all, training on the rifle range was the opportunity to fire live rounds. Practice using the .303 SMLE and a smaller-calibre .22 'miniature rifle' on the ranges ensured that all recruits received at least a grounding in musketry skills. In fact, to qualify as a 'trained soldier' a recruit must have undergone a system of training that involved shooting practice at a range of targets; this would vary according to the branch of service. Infantrymen (together with cavalrymen and sappers) required the greatest degree of training, involving the practice of grouping their shots, or of selective shooting at specific targets (known as 'application'). There were five components of training to be achieved before recruits could be considered as 'trained soldiers', picked out as 'Table A' (overleaf) in the regulations.

ABOVE Men of the Lonsdale Battalion (11th Border Regiment), Kitchener's Army, carry out musketry training, using Long Lees, under the watchful eye of their sergeant major, 1915.

TABLE A

PART I: INSTRUCTIONAL PRACTICES (ELEMENTARY)

No	Practice	Target	Distance (yds)	Rounds	Conduct of practice
1.	Grouping	2nd-class elementary (bullseye)	100	5	Lying, with arm or rifle rested
2.	Application	Ditto	200	5	Ditto
3.	Grouping	Ditto	100	5	Lying
4.	Application	Ditto	200	5	Lying
Total rounds				20	

PART II: INSTRUCTIONAL PRACTICES (REPETITION)

No	Practice	Target	Distance (yds)	Rounds	Conduct of practice
5.	Grouping	2nd-class elementary (bullseye)	100	5	Lying. All shots in 12in ring
6.	Application	2nd-class figure	200	5	Lying, with arm or rifle rested. Five hits, including four within inner (24in) ring
7.	Application	Ditto	200	5	Lying. Five hits within Magpie (36in) ring
8.	Application	Ditto	300	5	Lying. Five hits
9.	Application	1st-class figure	200	5	Kneeling. Four hits at least within inner (40in) ring
10.	Application	Ditto	300	5	Kneeling with arm or rifle rested. Four hits at least within inner (40in) ring
11.	Application	Ditto	400	5	Lying. Four hits at least
12.	Application	Ditto	500	5	Lying, with arm or rifle rested
13.	Application	Ditto	500	5	Lying
14.	Application	Ditto	600	5	Lying, with side of rifle only rested
Total rounds				50	

PART III: INSTRUCTIONAL PRACTICES (TIMED)

No	Practice	Target	Distance (yds)	Rounds	Conduct of practice
15.	Slow	2nd-class figure	200	5	Lying
16.	Slow	Ditto	200	5	Kneeling
17.	Rapid	Ditto	200	5	Lying. 40 seconds allowed
18.	Slow	1st-class figure	400	5	Lying
19.	Rapid	Ditto	400	5	Lying. 40 seconds allowed
20.	Slow	Ditto	300	5	Lying. Taking cover behind stones or sandbags representing a parapet and firing over them
21.	Snapshooting	2nd-class figure	200	5	Lying. Exposure, 6 seconds per shot
22.	Snapshooting	Ditto	500	5	Kneeling. Taking cover in a trench, or behind a screen representing a wall, and firing over the parapet. Exposure, 6 seconds for each shot.
Total rounds				40	

PART IV: INSTRUCTIONAL PRACTICES (CLASSIFICATION FOR SPECIAL RESERVE)

No	Practice	Target	Distance (yds)	Rounds	Conduct of practice
23.	Grouping	2nd-class elementary (bullseye)	100	5	Lying
24.	Application	1st-class figure	300	5	Kneeling
25.	Rapid	Ditto	300	5	Lying. 40 seconds allowed
26.	Snapshooting	2nd-class figure	200	5	Lying. Taking cover as in 20. Exposure, 5 seconds for each shot
27.	Application	1st-class figure	500	5	Lying
Total rounds				25	

PART V: INDIVIDUAL FIELD PRACTICES

Twenty rounds expended in elementary practices, ten rounds in an attack practice from 700 to 200yds, and ten rounds in a defence practice against full-length figures representing an advancing enemy.

Total rounds				20	

PART VI: COLLECTIVE FIELD PRACTICES

Twenty-five rounds will be expended, if ammunition available

Total rounds				25	
Surplus rounds				20	
Total rounds for Table A				200	

The diaries of Private Herbert Mason, a Kitchener volunteer with the 6th Battalion Oxfordshire and Buckinghamshire Light Infantry give a good indication of the instruction he received over two months in 1914–15, which included physical training, marching, tactical training and musketry. Private Mason left for France in July 1915.

Specialist training – for the coveted scout, signaller or expert marksman's proficiency badges, for example – would also be offered for

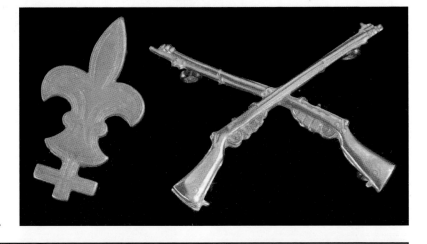

RIGHT Battalion scout and marksman badges.

PRIVATE H.T.N. MASON, 6TH BATTALION, OXFORDSHIRE AND BUCKINGHAMSHIRE LIGHT INFANTRY

Training diary, 1915

2 January	Arrived Blackdown Camp
6 January	Long route march, 9–5
7 January	Battalion Drill, 2–4; Trench digging 5–7
8 January	Company Drill, physical & musketry
9 January	Company Drill, then route march
11 January	Tactical [training] scheme
12 January	Battalion Drill
18 January	On miniature range
19 January	Battalion Drill
20 January	Battalion Drill; route march
21 January	Battalion Drill
22 January	Inspection by Kitchener
25–27 January	Out near Chobham Common
28 January	Short attack. Trench digging
29 January	Out on Chobham Common
30 January	Battalion Drill. Short attack then trench filling
1 February	Musketry miniature firing. Score 20/20, 5 bulls
2 February	Musketry miniature firing. Score 19/20, 5 bulls, 1 inner
3 February	Musketry, ball cartridge. Score 16/20, 2 inners, 1 outer, 2 bulls
4 February	Commenced firing course, 100yds grouping with rest, 8 in group, 20/20
5 February	Application 200yds rest, 16/20, plus 200yds without rest 15/20
7 February	Firing. 300yds lying, rest, 18/20; 300 kneeling, washout
8 February	500yds with rest, wind gauge altered 4 times and elevation once, 16/20
9 February	100yds lying, grouping 12 in, 15/25; 200yds lying, 13/20
10 February	Snap shooting, 200, 6 secs, 16/20. Didn't do 500yds due to light and wet
11 February	Fog prevented firing; short route march
12 February	100 yds grouping, 8 in, 20/25; snap shooting 5 secs, 16/20 200yds; rapid 8 per minute 18/32. Mist prevent[ed] firing at 500yds
13 February	Wet all day, no firing
15 February	Finished firing. 2 x 500yd practices. Route march
16 February	Route march. Town attack.
19 February	Shifted to Grayshott Camp
22 February	Battalion Drill. Skirmishing
24 February	Route march
25 February	Battalion attack Drill
26 February	Brigade route march
27 February	Kit inspection
1 March	Battalion Drill. Night Operations
2 March	Battalion Drill. Night Operations
3 March	Battalion Drill. Attack
9 March	Inspected by the King
10 March	Brigade Parade and training on Frensham Common
11 March	Brigade training on Frensham Common
12 March	Musketry and judging distances, night skirmishing
13 March	Kit Inspection
16 March	Brigade Parade
17 March	Brigade Parade
24 March	Divisional Parade
7 April	20th Division left for Larkshill

ABOVE Battalion scout, Loyal North Lancashire Regiment.

RIGHT 1907 Bayonet in 1914 Pattern leather equipment frog.

those of ability (Private Mason himself qualified as a scout); in return, as well as the badges, extra pay would be forthcoming. Variable in length, the average recruit would receive at least two months of training at home before leaving for the front. For later war recruits, weapons use was a significant component of the instruction, including the correct deployment of the Mills grenade – a function of the needs of trench warfare. Officers too would be expected to gain proficiency in arms. At late stages of the war, training also involved the acclimatisation to gas warfare – the correct fitting of the respirator, and the entry into gas chambers intended to check both the nerves of the wearer and the adequacy of the equipment. Left to the last was tutoring in the use of the bayonet in battle.

The bayonet

Bayonets have a long history in warfare, and mounted on the rifle were lineal descendants of such weapons as the spear and the pike. The use of the bayonet harks back to the application of such weapons in hand-to-hand combat that had been practised for millennia. Fitting the bayonet to his rifle linked the First World War soldier directly with this dark past, and of the reality of warfare itself.

For the British soldier, with the replacement of the long Lee-Enfield with the much shorter SMLE rifle in 1902 came the need for an extended bayonet. This was required as the likely enemy of the British soldier would be equipped with the longer Mauser-type rifle, meaning that he would be at a disadvantage in a lunging bayonet fight. The original bayonet issued with the long Lee-Enfield, and used with the bandolier equipment issued at the same time, was the 1903 pattern, at 12in in length, inadequate to counter the threat of German blades if used with the SMLE. As such, the 1907-pattern bayonet – always referred to as a 'sword' in British rifle regiments – was 5in longer than its predecessor; this would provide a reach comparable with any other existing weapons. The 1907-pattern bayonet attached to the SMLE by the use of a boss on the nose cap of the SMLE (beneath the muzzle), and a bayonet bar (officially known as the 'sword bar'), connecting with the mortise groove on the pommel of the bayonet. Early versions had hooked quillons; by 1914, this had been superseded by the simpler version with an uncomplicated crosspiece. Both versions had simple leather scabbards with steel top-mounts and tips (chapes) that were carried suspended from the belt by simple frogs.

For the average soldier, military instruction culminated in the use of the bayonet. At its simplest, bayonet training required the soldier to be able to fix and unfix his weapon while on parade; at its most complex, it involved charging at sacks marked with discs denoting head, eyes and heart, yelling like maniacs as they struck home. The emphasis on bayonet training remained undiminished throughout the war, and inculcating the 'spirit of the bayonet' was seen as essential in maintaining the martial stance of the British soldier.

Once fixed, the next motion was to unfix. This movement was somewhat more ungainly on the parade ground, but nevertheless essential if the soldier was not to fumble it on the battlefield.

FIXING BAYONETS FROM THE ORDER

From: *Infantry Training (4-Company Organisation), 1909* (reprinted with amendments 1914)

From the order position, bayonet fixing was carried out in a squad; on the command 'Fix' the right-hand man would take three paces forward; on the command 'Bayonets', the blade was withdrawn; after the third motion described below, he would return to his position. The man fixing his bayonet would turn his head to the right at step one, before returning it to the front in step three.

Fix bayonets – one
The handle of the bayonet is seized with the left hand, knuckles to the front, thumb and fingers to the rear; at the same time the muzzle of the rifle is pushed sharply forwards.

Fix bayonets – two
Taking time from the right-hand man in the squad, the bayonet is drawn, turning the point upwards and keeping the elbow down. The handle is placed on the bayonet standard of the rifle, with the ring in position over the stud on the nosecap, and the bayonet is pressed home to the catch; body and head erect.

Fix bayonets – three
Taking time from the right-hand man, the rifle is brought to the order; at the same time the left hand is cut away to the side.

The War Office manual *Bayonet Training, 1918* (reprinted with amendments 1916) made no bones about the purpose of bayonet fighting: 'hand-to-hand fighting with the bayonet is individual, which means that a man must think and act for himself and rely on his own resource and skill. ... In a bayonet assault all ranks go forward to kill, and only those who have developed skill and strength by constant training will be able to kill.' It was for this reason that army gymnastic trainers were consistent in developing in all soldiers what was known as the 'spirit of the bayonet'; an 'aggressive determination and confidence of superiority born of continual practice, without which a bayonet assault will not be effective'. Practice was everything, especially as the manual notes: 'To attack with the bayonet effectively requires good direction, strength and quickness, during a state of wild excitement and probably physical

UNFIXING BAYONETS

From: *Infantry Training (4-Company Organisation), 1909* (reprinted with amendments 1914)

From the order position, bayonet is fixed. As with bayonet fixing, unfixing on the parade ground is done in a squad. On the command 'Unfix', the left-hand man takes three paces forwards; on the command 'Bayonets' the first movement in this series is carried out. On completion of all four, the recruit returns to his position.

Unfix bayonets – one
With the heels closed, the rifle is placed between the knees, guard to the front. The handle of the bayonet is grasped with the right hand, knuckles to the front, the thumb of the left hand on the bayonet bolt spring. The rifle is then drawn into the body with the knees, and the spring pressed. The bayonet is then raised an inch to release it.

Unfix bayonets – two
Taking the time from the left-hand man, the bayonet is raised off the bayonet standard, and its point is dropped to the left side, ring to the rear. Raising the right hand, the scabbard is seized with the left hand, and the bayonet is guided into it.

Unfix bayonets – three
Taking time from the left-hand man, the bayonet is forced home, and the right hand is moved to the band of the rifle.

Unfix bayonets – four
Taking time from the left-hand man, the left hand is cut away to the side, and the soldier returns to the order.

exhaustion.' Instructors believed it would become second nature to the recruit.

Bayonet fighting was the culmination of the recruit's formal training, and it involved learning both the appropriate stances in order to repel a counter-charge, as well as the cold, unvarnished truth that a charge at the enemy will bring the soldier face to face with a man he would have to kill. The 'spirit of the bayonet' was in some ways central to the concept of the infantryman, soldiers required to close with the enemy and kill him. Instruction in handling the bayonet was therefore a psychological tool; if a man could be trained to use the bayonet, he could also be taught to kill his opponent. The limit of the range of the bayonet was reckoned to be around 5ft; killing was expected to be at close quarters, at a range of around 2ft, 'when troops are struggling *corps à corps* in trenches or darkness'. But the first lesson in any training was the adoption of the appropriate balanced stances from which to launch an attack, or even to deflect an opponent's lunge towards you.

The drill aspects of bayonet fighting could be taught with instructor and recruit, and getting the correct stances was more a feature of stability and confidence. Ensuring that the bayonet reached its target and did its job was essential, as with the point. *Bayonet Training 1918* was clear on this: 'The point of the bayonet should be directed against an opponent's throat, especially in *corps à corps* fighting, as the point will enter easily and make a fatal wound on penetrating a few inches and, being near the eyes, makes an opponent "funk".' This focus on the throat was amplified by the inclusion of an additional stance in the training – the jab. The jab required the recruit to use his weapon at close quarters, developing a short point into a vertical movement whereby the bayonet was thrust upwards into the chin of his enemy, rapidly disabling him. Parrying, the act of forcing away the enemy's own bayonet thrusts also demanded confidence. Drill instructors were equipped with a parrying stick; a length of cane with a pad at one end and a loop at the other. Into the loop recruits were invited to thrust their bayonets by the instructor; the pad allowed him to parry away thrusts and to invite the recruit to attack it with the butt of his rifle.

ABOVE Bayonet training; use of the parry stick.

The final component of training, the assault, required the soldier to charge an opponent and stab him with his bayonet. Men were sufficiently worked up to carry out this duty on prepared sacks suspended from frames, as if they were enemy soldiers; if the 'spirit of the bayonet' could be sufficiently inculcated, then the actual act of the charge in action might appear less terrifying. With the possibility of soldiers injuring themselves or others during this assault, the bayonet charge was not held until the recruit was sufficiently versed in bayonet training. As the war progressed, so the instruction became more focused on clearing enemy positions: *Bayonet Training 1918* recommended attacks across shelled terrain, against entrenched lines manned with sacks and dummies. Early in the war, charging against suspended sacks was more the norm. The sacks were filled with vertical layers of straw and thin sods; upright pieces of wood were sometimes inserted in order to replicate a bayonet point meeting resistance, as if striking bone.

BAYONET TRAINING STANCES

From: Infantry Training (4-Company Organisation), 1909 (reprinted with amendments 1914)

Adopting the correct stance in bayonet fighting was essential.

'On Guard' **[1]**
Starting from the position 'Order Arms' the rifle is canted forwards with the bayonet to the front, held as high as the breast, the barrel inclined to the left seized with the left hand below the band, though not below the back-sight, the right hand, just in advance of the hip, grasping the small of the rifle. The legs are kept in a natural position as if walking. 'On Guard' was the starting point for all bayonet exercises, and was intended to represent 'aggression, alertness and readiness to go forward for immediate attack'.

Rest
The position of rest can be assumed from any of the drill stances, and without unnecessary drill.

The point **[2]**
From the 'On Guard' position, the point of the bayonet is thrust as rapidly as possible anywhere to the trunk of the opponent, to the full extent of the arms; the point is then withdrawn at once. The body should be inclined forwards to ensure its weight is behind the point, and the left knee is slightly bent when delivering it.

Right parry **[3]**
From the 'On Guard' position, the rifle is carried sufficiently to the right front, straightening the left arm in doing so,

THE BAYONET CHARGE

From: *Infantry Training (4-Company Organisation), 1909* (reprinted with amendments 1914)

The bayonet charge was made against sacks and was launched from the 'On Guard' position. This series of images shows the recruit rushing towards a sack suspended from a wooden gallows. Grimacing with his 'war face' and yelling, he charges in a state of high excitement. The point of the bayonet is forced into the sack; the tilt guarantees that the blade penetrates the body and is not stopped by the ribs. Making certain that the bayonet is not pressed home to such an extent that a quick withdrawal is difficult, the recruit removes the bayonet from his target. The purpose of the assault is to ensure that the enemy is killed with the bayonet alone.

so as to beat off the enemy's rifle to the right. The rifle is held with a straight wrist.

Left parry **[4]**

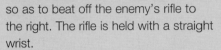

From the 'On Guard' position, the rifle is carried sufficiently to the left front, straightening the left arm in doing so, so as to beat off an enemy's rifle towards the left front; or to the left front and downwards when the parry is a low one. The rifle is held with a straight wrist.

Shorten arm **[5]**
From the 'On Guard' position, draw the rifle sharply back on the horizontal to the full extent of the right arm, with the butt of the rifle either above or below the elbow. The point is then delivered from this position; the purpose of this move is to allow a soldier to deliver the point when close to the enemy.

The butt **[6]**
Use of the butt is a secondary attack following a failed point or a parried

thrust. Other secondary attacks could be tripping, or bringing the knee up sharply will also help, though the brass-bound butt is a significant blunt instrument. The butt is used by raising it forward and upward with the right hand, while drawing the barrel over the shoulder.

Tripping
Any form of tripping is followed by the use of the butt, though this is not something that can be practised directly.

Chapter Three

Trenches and trench routine

For most soldiers, serving in the front line meant serving 'in the trenches, somewhere in France'. The trench lines in Western Europe stretched from the Swiss Frontier to the North Sea with the British soldier placed squarely on the right flank of the German line, protecting the channel ports, and the route to Paris.

OPPOSITE Men of the Royal West Kent Regiment in the trenches, c.1916.

For most British soldiers, trench warfare was to be the norm, even in far-flung theatres such as Gallipoli and Salonika. Despised by the army High Command as a 'phase of warfare' that would soon be transformed into open warfare, 'the trenches' would exist from their first inception in September 1914 through to the opening of the Battle of Amiens in August 1918, and the final advance to victory. The reasons why trench warfare developed were succinctly put in an official manual *Notes for Infantry Officers on Trench Warfare*, published in March 1916, and issued to officers in training – men who were likely to see action in the largest British offensive to date, the Battle of the Somme in July 1916. This manual asserted that, 'it must be clearly understood that trench fighting is only a phase of operations, and that instruction in the subject, essential as it is, is only one branch of the training of troops'. The manual went further in describing 'the special conditions' that led to the creation of trench warfare.

As described in the manual, the Western Front – so described because it represented the western theatre of operations of the German army, which was fighting in the east on a two-front war – became an entity once the opposing forces had entrenched across northern Europe, in late 1914. It was on the Western Front that trenches became the dominant feature of warfare. The importance of massed artillery and the firepower that could be brought to bear by the infantryman or by machine guns was testimony to that. Men naturally went to ground, and in so doing pitted the artilleryman against the engineer. In truth, the only way that this situation could change was through reliance on the only arm capable of effecting it – the infantry, who ultimately would have to rise from the trenches in a frontal assault. Once the trench

BELOW The trenches; German cavalry ride by a section of disused British trenches on the Western Front.

CONSIDERATIONS AFFECTING DESIGN OF DEFENCES

From: *Notes for Infantry Officers on Trench Warfare* (1916)

Three facts in particular give to modern trench fighting under present conditions most of its special characteristics. These are:

A The continual proximity of the opposing forces;
B The length of time for which they have generally occupied the same ground;
C The fact that neither side has a flank so long as it remains on the defensive, so that every attack must be frontal.

As a result of the length of time the opposing forces have been in close proximity on practically the same ground, the original trenches dug at the end of the period of manoeuvre operations have grown into a complicated system of entrenchments. The design and organisation of these have been influenced by the nature of the artillery, up to calibres far heavier than could be utilised in ordinary field operations.

The rapidity with which artillery can form a barrage to meet an attack makes it necessary that the moment of the assault should come as a surprise, and the trenches from which an attack is to be made should therefore be within close assaulting distance of the opposing front line.

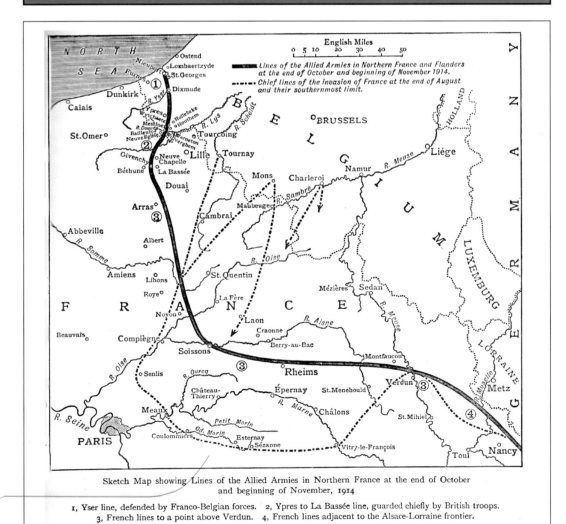

Sketch Map showing Lines of the Allied Armies in Northern France at the end of October and beginning of November, 1914

1, Yser line, defended by Franco-Belgian forces.   2, Ypres to La Bassée line, guarded chiefly by British troops.
3, French lines to a point above Verdun.   4, French lines adjacent to the Alsace-Lorraine frontier.

LEFT The trench positions on the Western Front from the Swiss Frontier to the North Sea, largely fixed in position after the battles for position during the 'race for the sea', in the autumn of 1914.

ABOVE **The Belgian city of Ypres, protected from capture for four years, but shelled to rubble.**

lines reached practically unbroken from the sea to the small village of Pfetterhouse on the Swiss border, outflanking movements were no longer an option, and the stalemate of 'the trenches' became standard for four long years of war.

The Western Front crossed France and into Belgium and represented the stabilised front that had been formed after the German plan to knock France out of the war by the great swinging motion of its armies – the Schlieffen Plan – had failed. The Germans were held on the line of the Marne River just west of Paris, after the momentum of the German assault faltered in August–September 1914. From here the opportunity for the opposing armies to outflank each other was lost, and each side raced ever closer to the coast in an attempt to do just that. The 'race for the sea' became a closing door that committed both sides to the trench warfare that was to rage on for four years. This front became a continuous line of trenches from Switzerland to the North Sea, 475 miles across varied terrain, the largest fortification in history, the greatest siege operation ever committed.

For the British soldier the Western Front was taken to mean that portion of France and Flanders that extended from St Quentin in France in the south, to just north of the Belgian town of Ypres, now known by its Flemish name of Leper. By the end of the war British and Commonwealth troops were to occupy some 120 miles of the front, in the historically strategic zone that straddled the Belgo-French border, extending south deep into Picardy. Arriving in early August 1914, the British Expeditionary Force took its place alongside the French in defending the line, and were almost immediately repelled, withdrawing with the French to the line of the River Aisne, taking part in the spirited defence that would become known as the

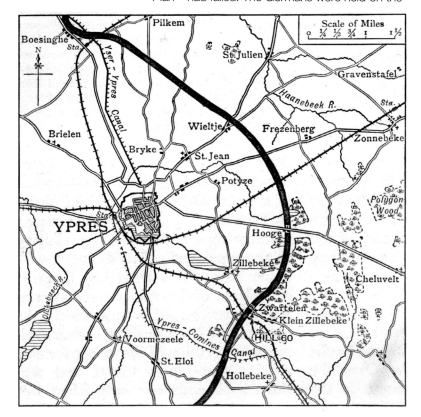

LEFT **The Ypres Salient was a bulge in the line that protected the city of Ypres. The Germans held the high ground to the east of the city, and bombarded it mercilessly.**

miracle of the Marne. The aftermath of the Marne was a battle that would push back the German tide and see the formulation of the Western Front. With 1914 drawing to a close, the British took up their positions north of Armentières. Here developed the bulge in the line that would become known as the Ypres salient, defending the last sizeable city to be left in Allied hands: after all Britain had joined the fight to protect 'Gallant Little Belgium'.

With Ypres destined to be defended at all costs, the salient would see four major battles, and very many smaller conflicts and personal tragedies. The city would never fall, but at great human loss, and the images of the trench warfare carried out in this sector have become visual metaphors of the whole war. Further south, the line snaked though French Flanders to Artois, and the city of Arras. Like Ypres, Arras would become a British city during the war. Above ground and below it, British and Commonwealth troops lived, worked and fought to protect this ancient city. For many, though, it is the Somme that represents the greatest focal point for British involvement on the Western Front. Taken over from the French in May 1915, the line of the Somme battlefield, from Maricourt in the south to Gommecourt in the north, was the scene of one of the most costly battles in British military history, when men of Kitchener's Army rose out of their trenches on 1 July 1916 to face the heavily entrenched might of the Imperial German army. Up and down the old battlefront, small battlefield cemeteries are testament to the level of sacrifice. Over four years of war, the British Expeditionary Force was locked into a largely static siege war on a limited front. Although the offensives of 1915, 1916 and 1917 all started with the hopes that this might change, it was the titanic battle of 1918, the offensive of the Hundred Days, that would see Allied armies – with the BEF at the heart – push back the Germans day –after day to defeat, symbolically ending the war on 11 November 1918 where it had started, in the Belgian town of Mons.

RIGHT The extension of the British Line southwards from the city of Arras in 1916; the British took over the Somme Front in May 1916 in preparation for the great offensive.

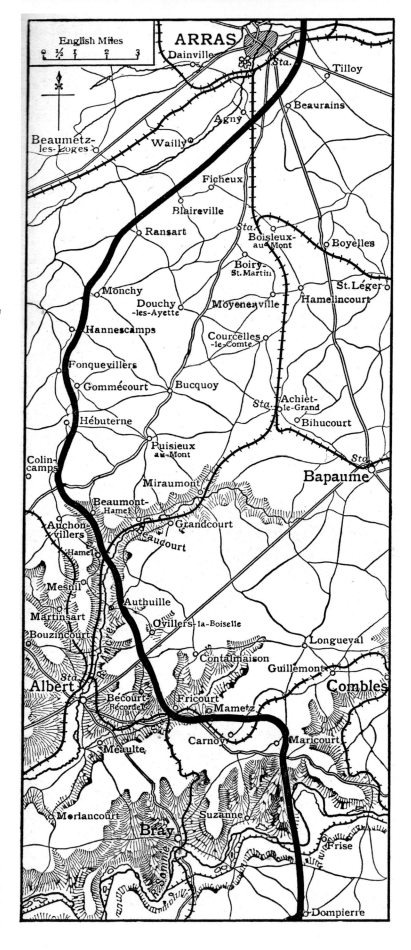

ABOVE **British trench in c.1915; narrow, and well supported by sandbags.**

The trench

In their simplest sense, trenches were linear excavations of variable depth that were mostly open to the sky, but were sometimes roofed for concealment purposes, usually with close-boarded timber – however, this was rare. The stated purpose of the trenches was, of course, to provide protection to the front-line troops and their supporting arms in the face of small-arms fire (rifles, machine guns etc) and artillery.

Despite their simplicity, the function of trenches varied and as the war progressed with no absolute sign of a break in the deadlock, more and more types were developed. However, in the main there were two consistent configurations: fire trenches, which formed the front lines, and communication trenches, which joined them. Fire trenches (ie fighting trenches) were divided into a regular pattern of fire bays and traverses, which meant that no soldier could walk in a straight line for long, without having to switch back on himself. This was intended to limit the effects of shellfire, or rifle and machine-

CONSTRUCTIONAL DETAILS OF TRENCHES

From: *Notes for Infantry Officers on Trench Warfare* (1916)

Fire trenches
There is no standard pattern of fire trench, and the type used varies according to local conditions. There are a number of essential conditions that a fire trench must fulfil, however:

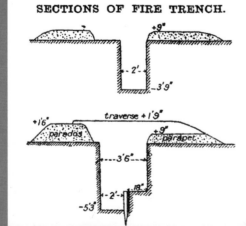

ABOVE **Standard dimensions for a British Fire Trench in 1916, showing the parapet and parados, and firestep.**

A The parapet must be bullet-proof;
B Every man must be able to fire over the parapet with proper effect (ie so that he can hit the bottom of his own wire);
C The narrower the trench, the better the cover it affords; a fire trench should be wide enough for men to fire over the parapet with others passing behind them;
D Traverses must be adequate;
E A parados must be provided to give protection against the back-blast of high explosive;
F The trace of the trench should be irregular, to provide flanking fire;
G If the trench is held for any length of time, the sides must be revetted; and
H The bottom of the trench must be floored.

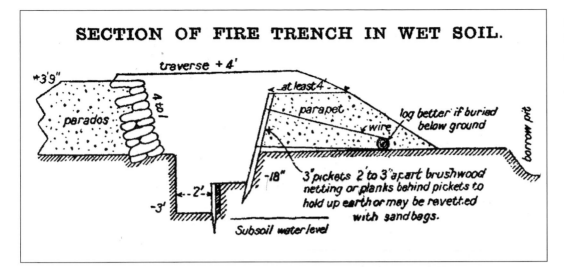

SECTION OF FIRE TRENCH IN WET SOIL.

traverse + 4'

+3'9"

parados

at least 4

parapet

log better if buried below ground

wire

borrow pit

-18"

-2'

-3'

3' pickets 2' to 3' apart brushwood netting or planks behind pickets to hold up earth or may be revetted with sandbags.

Subsoil water level

LEFT Trench section in wet ground. Here it was necessary to build upwards, using sandbags and other materials.

gun fire along the length of a trench – with the inevitable consequences. British and German fire trenches were alike in this respect; French versions often had a more leisurely, curved form of zigzag. In fact French military engineering was the inspiration for much of trench warfare, and French terms were commonly applied. Thus, the spoil removed in digging a trench was used to form a *parapet* – a mound of earth in front of the trench on the enemy side, intended to stop bullets, and a *parados* – a slightly higher mound at the rear, which would interrupt the movement of bullets, and prevent soldiers' heads from being silhouetted against the skyline. Loopholes were provided to observe the enemy; found as steel plates with a hole big enough to admit a rifle, they were often targeted by snipers. Because of this, blankets and other coverings were used to create darkness behind them.

For the most part, fire trenches were between 6ft and 8ft deep, with a prescribed depth, according to High Command, being 5ft 9in in dry soil, with a further 9in of soil built up as a parapet, preferably in an irregular form to confuse the enemy observers. In areas where groundwater was close to surface, 'borrow pits' were dug on either side of the trench to supply extra earth needed to build up a sufficient height to protect the troops. Each fire trench was equipped with a fire step, ideally of regulation 2ft high and 18in wide, sufficient to raise an average man's head above the protection of the parapet, when required to do so.

Excavating this depth of trench was the ideal, although in some cases it was impossible to dig

LOOPHOLES

From: Notes for Infantry Officers on Trench Warfare (1916)

ABOVE Steel loophole plate; the loophole itself was covered by a steel door.

All firing by night, and to meet an attack whether by day or night, must be over the top of the parapet. In all fire trenches, however, a certain number of loopholes are necessary for the use of snipers to inflict casualties on the enemy whenever opportunity offers, to annoy him, interfere with his work, keep him under cover, and keep down the fire of his snipers. Usually one or two loopholes are made in each bay of the fire trenches.

The maximum amount of cover should be provided for the firer, and the steel loophole plates with a metal flap to close the loophole make probably the best form. Loopholes should have a curtain (sandbag or some form of cloth) hung on the firer's side, to be used in the same way as a photographer uses a black cloth.

RECONSTRUCTED TRENCHES

Although trenches were common scars in the landscape of northern France and Belgium for many years after the war had ended, the majority have now melted away into the ground, ploughed back to their origins. Some survive, maintained as living museums. In other cases, reconstructions have been built to standard specification in order to illustrate the nature of trench warfare.

ABOVE Sanctuary Wood: reconstructed trenches in the Ypres Salient.

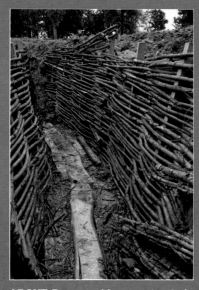

ABOVE Bayernwald, reconstructed German trenches in the Ypres Salient.

ABOVE Reconstructed trench showing trench boarding and firestep, with trench ladder in position.

Sanctuary Wood, Ypres Salient
Preserved in the Ypres Salient, these British and Canadian trenches follow the traces of actual examples, and are authentic in their layout. The revetment and flooring are reconstructions but sympathetically done. The Sanctuary Wood trenches show the typical trace of those close to the front line; however, these are not 'organised for fire' with fire steps – they are shallower than would have been seen in action; parapets and parados would have been built up using sandbags.

Bayernwald, Ypres Salient
Bayernwald is a set of German trenches developed along the line of original front-line trench systems in the area of Wychshaete, in the Ypres Salient. Illustrated are S-shaped communication trenches, designed to allow the movement of stretcher-bearers to and from the front line. The use of wattle revetments is typical of German trenches, as is the use of planking in the bottom. These are full-depth trenches.

Reconstructed front-line trenches
Both trench types illustrated in these reconstructions show the fire step. The use of a fire step allowed the soldier to raise his head up to a firing position; and by standing in the centre of the trench meant he could keep his head out of the firing zone, below the parapet. The idea of the parados was to prevent soldiers' heads being silhouetted against the skyline, thereby being targeted by snipers. The parapet was there to protect the soldier; where the parapet was in poor condition, soldiers were in danger of being picked off. Both examples show different construction methods. Timber revetments protected the trench slopes, and were held in position using angle iron that was secured to logs or other anchor points buried in the slopes. Both examples give a good idea of well-constructed trenches in c.1916.

more than a foot or so before reaching water-saturated ground, especially in the Ypres salient, with its underlying foundation of water-repelling clay. Here, instead, the trenches were built up rather than dug down, creating what was known as 'High Command' or 'Parapet' trenches, usually with walls of the ubiquitous sandbags filled with whatever was closest to hand, but preferably sandy soils capable of stopping the rounds that buzzed across no-man's-land. In other situations, boxes or gabions were used as the basis for the parapet. In order to achieve this, specially constructed inverted 'A' frames were manufactured in order to support both the sloping walls of the trenches, and the duckboard flooring.

Trench sides (known as slopes) were supported or 'revetted' with whatever was available, sometimes wattle, often corrugated sheeting and expanded metal (xpm), occasionally chicken wire, or even timber boards if obtainable. Timber was universally used to hold these materials in place, anchored deep into the earth, and layers of bonded sandbags strengthened the whole.

ABOVE The wet ground of Flanders: after the Third Battle of Ypres the ground conditions were poor. Duckboard tracks were used to move across the battlefield.

LEFT Close-boarded trenches showing firestep.

RIGHT A journalist visits British trenches on the Somme, 1917. The trenches are narrow, solidly revetted with timber, and built up with sandbags.

BELOW An empty Great War period sandbag recovered from a tunnel on the Western Front.

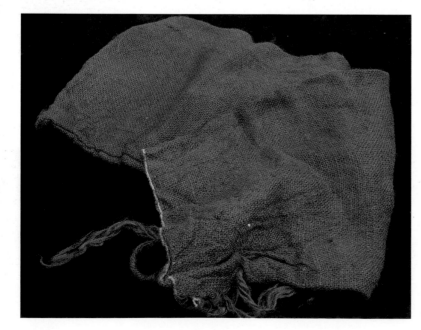

Recent archaeology in Flanders has uncovered the remains of these in situ, and has supported the notion of a constant battle between man and nature in keeping the trenches in some kind of order – essential for the maintenance of morale, and the adequate protection of their soldiery.

Most trenches were 'floored' with wooden duckboards, which were built up to allow drainage beneath – in fact it was common for successive levels of duckboards to be laid one on top of another to combat the difficult conditions encountered. In rare cases, bricks and rubble were used, when trench lines snaked through destroyed villages and houses. Ensuring the trench was adequately drained and floored in this way was essential, if the men were not to suffer from the elements, as well as the constant shellfire.

REVETMENT

From: Notes for Infantry Officers on Trench Warfare (1916)

The side of trenches which have to be occupied for a long time, and particularly in wet weather on a damp site, must be revetted. Hurdles or rabbit netting held up by stout stakes securely wired to short pickets firmly anchored in the parapet or parados, form a useful type of revetment for this purpose. Sandbags are not so suitable. In the winter in Flanders some really solid form of revetment, such as planks or timber, or expanded metal sheets, is necessary.

ARCHAEOLOGY OF THE TRENCHES

The Ypres Salient has seen a number of archaeological investigations in recent years that has uncovered the nature of the trenches and of the need to control the damp ground conditions that would plague the average infantryman.

The top image shows a portion of a front line trench excavated on the north limb of the Ypres Salient. Here, with ground conditions particularly treacherous, and with the possibility of flooding a constant hazard, ensuring that trenches were both adequately drained and securely revetted was essential so that they could survive the adverse attentions of both the weather conditions and the German artillery. This trench (right) dates from c1917, and the archaeological investigations show how the trench shifts sharply in direction, dividing it into traverses and fire bays. This limited the effects of shelling and of machine-gun fire along its length. Maintaining the slopes of the trenches are corrugated-iron sheeting held in place by wooden beams at regular intervals. In fact, these beams are part of an inverted 'A Frame', the cross bar of each 'A' being clearly seen. The purpose of these frames was to provide support for the trench slopes, and to allow for the construction of duckboards that were held above the normal level of water that would naturally accumulate in this ditch over a year. The trench required sandbags to build up the parapet and thereby protect its occupants; 'fossilised' examples have been found in situ in such excavations.

The lower image shows a portion of German front-line trench that was captured by the British in 1917, during the Battle of Messines. Situated in Messines itself, the German occupiers had opportunity to recover timbers, doors and other materials in order to revet and support their trench slopes. Also demonstrating a traverse to prevent enfilade fire, the excavation revealed a green-painted door reused as a trench board. The trench slopes and its sides are supported by thick tree branches and stakes, and along its length a variety of revetment types have been used, including wattle. The trench is floored by boards crossing the trench, laid on top of successive layers in order to try and escape from the pervasive dampness. Once again, the parapet and parados needed building up to protect its occupants; digging down into the wet soils was not a viable option.

ABOVE British frontline trench excavated in the northern Ypres Salient, showing the construction with A-frames and corrugated sheeting.

BELOW German frontline trench in Messines, Ypres Salient, showing the reuse of timbers recovered from destroyed buildings.

ORGANISATION OF DEFENSIVE LINE

From: *Knowledge for War. Every Officer's Handbook for the Front* (1916)

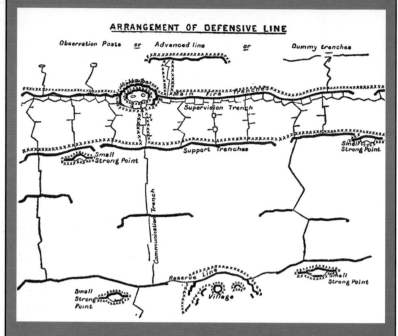

ABOVE Diagram of the mid-war trench system, showing the front, support and reserve trenches, and the connecting Communication Trenches, or CTs.

The following summary will give a good general idea of the means taken to prepare a defensive front in trench warfare:

A Obstacles – generally barbed wire – in front of first-line trench, concealed if possible from artillery observation.

B Listening posts, lookout posts, machine guns.

C Fire trenches, recessed and traversed.

D Communication trenches to the rear, linking up the whole system.

E Shelters and dugouts. These should be immediately behind the first-line fire trenches, with easy communication to them.

F Support trenches – traversed – from 25 to 100yds in rear of fire trenches.

G Dressing stations, kitchen, etc, branching from communication trenches.

H Second-line trenches. Fire trenches, machine guns, etc, similar to organisation of first line.

I Supporting points, behind second line, well defended by parties of 20 to 40 men, serve to hold up enemy assault on first and second lines; such points should be entirely surrounded by barbed wire.

The trench system

A commercially produced manual, *Knowledge for War. Every Officer's Handbook for the Front*, published in 1916, gives a list of the principal components of a trench system at this midpoint in the war, a complex arrangement of lines to give the maximum confidence of 'defence in depth'.

Fire trenches were usually arranged in successive parallel rows, with the front line, support line and reserve line all connected by the communication trenches, which were the main thoroughfares of trench warfare. In well-established trench systems the front line consisted of a fire trench and ancillary supervision trench with deeper dugouts providing accommodation for the troops. This ideal represented the idea of defence in depth; as the war progressed beyond 1916 so increasingly the front became more fluid, especially as the front line was obviously most often targeted by the enemy artillery. Late in the war, front lines became outposts. Few men served in these; instead there was a small garrison intended to interrupt the initial assault and to brave the shells.

Behind the front line were the support and reserve lines, trenches that were still 'organised for fire' with the intention of holding back the enemy if a breakthrough of the front line had been achieved. Most important was the support line, as it was here that the major part of the trench garrison was housed, with a smaller number of sentries in the front line itself. Further back were the reserve lines, housing men who had been cycled out of the front line, taking their turn before they were removed from the line completely for a period of rest.

The purpose of communication trenches (or 'CTs') was to link the forward or fire trenches to the reserve lines and beyond to the rear areas, and to allow men, munitions and supplies to travel up to the line – as well as wounded soldiers to come out of it. For this reason, they were wide enough to allow stretcher-bearers to carry out their duties. Very often these long trenches bore names such as 'alley', 'lane' or 'street', indicating their intended purpose. Communication trenches were usually dug in a zigzag or wavy pattern, and in Flanders, where the geological conditions meant that revetment was essential, they had

THE FRONT LINE

From: *Notes for Infantry Officers on Trench Warfare* (1916)

The front line generally consists of two parts, the fire trench and the command or supervision trench. The fire trench may either be a continuous trench (although in no case should it be an absolutely straight one), traversed at suitable intervals to give protection from enfilade fire and to localise the effect of shell bursts, or may consist of fire bays, T-shaped or L-shaped in plan, jutting forward from the supervision trench. The latter is a continuous trench affording easy lateral communication close behind the fire bays or fire trench, and connected with them at frequent intervals.

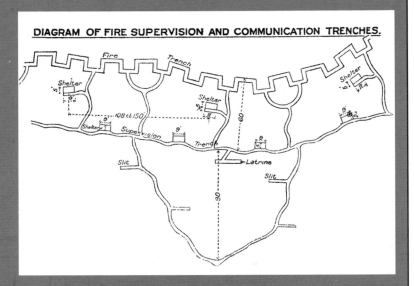

ABOVE Idealised diagram of the frontline with its supervision trench behind.

BELOW A famous image from the Great War; British soldiers in the captured German trenches at Orvilliers, on the Somme, in 1916. As these are German trenches, the sleeping men lie on the original firestep, while the sentry has had to improvise. 'Turning' trenches like this required men to carry digging tools when going 'over the top'.

SUPPORT AND RESERVE TRENCHES

From: *Notes for Infantry Officers on Trench Warfare* (1916)

Support trenches

The support trenches accommodate the first support to the garrison of the front trench, ready for immediate reinforcement or local counter-attack; they also provide cover to which the bulk of the garrison of the front line can be withdrawn when it is under bombardment. The support line is constructed as a second line of resistance, if the first line is lost, and should be protected by an obstacle. In order that support trenches may not suffer the bombardment of the front line they should not be nearer than 50yds behind it, the most favourable position being 70–100yds behind. Support trenches should be designed as traversed fire trenches, but the supervision trench is usually omitted.

Reserve line

Behind the support trenches, and also connected with them using communication trenches, lies the reserve line, which may consist of a line of trenches but more usually of dugouts, often formed by improving the cover of a natural feature. The reserve lines are to accommodate the battalion reserve, whose purpose is the local counter-attack. The reserve line may be some 400–600yds from the rear of the front line.

similar dimensions to a fire trench. In some cases (such as at Arras, and Nieuport on the Belgian coast), CTs were replaced by underground subways, which provided much more protection from the searching of enemy artillery.

Most soldiers would travel to the front line from the rear areas along crowded CTs at night: bustling, narrow thoroughfares 6ft deep with barely enough room for men to pass. Although relieving battalions would be guided to the front by experienced soldiers from the battalion about to be relieved, to direct them, signboards would still be necessary, picked out by candlelight. Like the front lines, many of the long CTs had picturesque names, chosen at will and whim; these would be painted on rough and crude boards to aid in direction finding. Such boards would also exist in the front line; and others, with a more urgent message, might warn of the dangers from snipers, artillery fire or the physical hazards of loose or low wires, or treacherous duckboards.

The height of advancement in the trench system was achieved in the mid-part of the war; and the intricacies of the system would be recorded on equally complex trench maps. Yet, at first, British trench maps showed only German

RIGHT Digging a communication trench through Delville Wood. Battle of Bazentin Ridge, 14–17 July 1916.

trench lines, for fear of them falling into enemy hands. It was only late on in the war that they would appear alongside the enemy lines on these valuable documents. With this in mind, and due to the complexities of the growing trench lines, it was possible to get hopelessly lost, and trench signboards were fixed to allow newcomers to a particular stretch to get orientated. Trenches were named or numbered, according to the preference of the commanders in charge, and were often themed – with matching initial letters, the names of towns of villages, or common city streets being typical. In most cases, it was necessary to direct soldiers through the maze of trenches, for although they were theoretically constructed in parallel lines – at least in the early stages of trench warfare on the Western Front – the re-entrants, salients and redoubts would be interconnected by communication trenches and have minor trenches intended as latrines, entrances to dugouts, trench mortar batteries, and so on. This created a confusing mess of ditches to trap the unwary.

Escaping the open ditches required going to ground, though there was official antipathy

ABOVE British trench map of the Wytschaete area, Ypres Salient. The German trenches are shown (in red); the British frontline is denoted by a blue line.

BELOW Australian stretcher-bearers in a support trench, each with his own 'cubby' or 'funk-hole'.

to dugouts, for fear that the men may never emerge from them to face the assault. Despite this, throughout the war dugouts were to evolve from simple scrapes in the trench slopes known to the men as 'funk' or 'cubby' holes, providing little more than limited cover – and often requiring the occupant to stretch his legs out into the main trench line – to deeper affairs dug or 'mined' to provide protection from the attentions of howitzer shells and trench mortars. In most cases, accommodation was still squalid, despite the welcome protection it provided.

Deep dugouts were encountered by the British in northern France, when, in the aftermath of the Battles of Loos (September 1915) and the Somme (July–November 1916) they discovered the Germans had dug deep, dry shelters in the hard chalk. Ironically, the Germans had fewer opportunities for digging deep dugouts in the Ypres salient, due to unfavourable water-bearing layers at the top of the hills they occupied that faced the city. Concrete 'pill boxes' or MEBU (*Mannschafts Eisenbeton Unterstanden*) were the German solution in this wet ground. For the British, positioned on clays in the low slopes around Ypres that were for all intents and purposes

the same as those under London, there was the possibility of mined bombproof shelters, clay being the perfect material to dig into – so long as there were sufficient supports available. As this was the case, and with mounting losses, common sense prevailed, fortunately, and deeper dugouts started appearing in the British lines from the end of 1915 onwards, for accommodation, headquarters space, and regimental aid posts. By the end of the war the British had provided quarters for thousands of men across their frontage, the antipathy of the High Command evaporating in 1917.

Digging trenches

Trenches were laid out by the Royal Engineers – that most versatile corps of the British Army – but were dug by the infantry. In fact, some 68 infantry battalions would be transformed into pioneers, and each division received one of these newly designated units. Men of the Pioneer Battalions – distinguished by their crossed rife and pick collar badges – were equipped and trained as fighting soldiers, but were skilled enough to provide essential labour, building roads, excavating dugouts and maintaining services. Later in the war, medically downgraded men – often men recovered from wounds or illness – would be transferred into the Labour Corps to provide an essential workforce in the rear areas. They too would be called upon to fight in an emergency.

Yet despite their specialists, no infantryman could escape digging. All were equipped with a clever personal entrenching tool, which comprised a steel head of combined spade and pick, and a separate wooden handle, called a helve. These tools provided a means of digging a shallow scrape in an emergency, or were used for a multitude of other small jobs in the field, acting as hammer, pick and digging tool. The tool was supplied principally for men caught in the open and faced with incoming fire, as described by Captain B.C. Lake in his 1916 guide *Knowledge of War. Every Officer's Handbook for the Front*.

It is doubtful that entrenching tools were used to dig many trenches; for that the ubiquitous General Service (GS) spades were needed. These versatile tools were issued to the

ABOVE Soldier using the pick of his entrenching tool to break up the ground.

BELOW General Service spades. The one at the top of the pile, recovered from the Arras battlefield, has received a bullet hole.

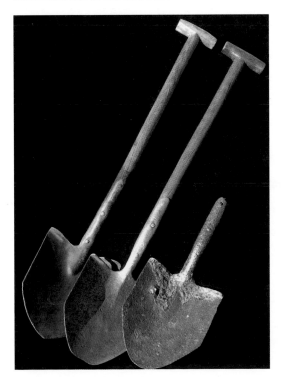

USE OF THE ENTRENCHING TOOL OR 'GRUBBER'

From: *Knowledge of War. Every Officer's Handbook for the Front* (1916)

Men to wait for orders. There should be no entrenching so long as there is a possibility of closing with the enemy and using the bayonet.

The spade of the 'grubber' was used to build up cover for the rifleman.

A Magazines must be fully charged and cartridge pouches fastened. Rifles a full arm's length to the right, muzzle to the front.

B Men get out the grubber. Tear up and collect any vegetation within arm's length, and heap it loosely as a screen.

C Use pick or blade according to hardness of ground. Hack a loose furrow 1½ft to right as far as possible forward and backward.

D Hold grubber by handle close to its head. Use blade as scoop or hoe. Scoop loose earth out of furrow and heap it up close in front of left eye and shoulder.

E Each new lot of loose earth to thicken parapet to be put in direct line between head of man and point from which fire seems to come.

F Deepen 6in in front, 12in rear end, and make a parapet 6in high.

G Men must be ready to lay down grubber and resume firing at any stage.

battalion at the rate of 110 per battalion; open-mouthed, with a turned-back top to protect the shovel from the heavy boot of the infantryman, they were used in earnest in the excavation of front-line trenches.

The time estimated in 1914 (as prescribed by the officer's *Field Service Pocket Book, 1914*) for digging a man's length of fire trench – two paces or 45cu ft – was 100 minutes under normal conditions. Heavy picks were also provided, with 76 issued per battalion, and were there to break the ground so the spademen could do their work. The use of picks over spades depended very strongly upon the nature of the ground. Both tools would be used in hollowing out trenches throughout the war; under the orders of sapper officers and NCOs, the infantry would provide the manpower to do so.

Infantrymen were often to carry spades (and picks) into action, most famously by the leading assault troops on the Somme in 1916. This was to allow for the 'turning' of trench lines once captured, with the reversal of the fire step

TRENCH DIGGING

From: *Manual of Field Engineering, 1911* (reprinted 1913)

The design of a trench will depend on the time and labour available, on the soil, on the site, and on the range and description of fire which may be brought to bear on it, but the following rules are common to all:

A The parapet should be bulletproof at the top.
B The parapet and trench should be as inconspicuous as possible.
C The interior slope should be as steep as possible.
D The trench should be wide enough to admit of the passage of a stretcher without interfering with the men firing.
E The interior of the trench should be protected, as far as possible, against oblique and enfilade fire.
F Arrangements for drainage should be made.

To excavate a length of 2 paces per digger of a trench will take an untrained man 1½ hours, in moderately easy ground.

RIGHT The GS shovel in action in extending a vulnerable trench line.

from one side to the other. In this way, enemy trenches could be turned against their former occupants, and help to stave off the inevitable counter-attacks.

Barbed wire and no-man's-land

Between the front lines of the opposing trenches was 'no-man's-land', a strip of contested ground that varied in width from a few feet to tens of yards. The term was coined early in the war, but had already had a long history as the name for a 'forbidding place'. It was certainly that: the dead ground between the opposing trenches that was bordered by dense thickets of barbed wire was an unwelcoming place, particularly if the ground had been a silent witness to a raid or attack 'over the bags'.

Tactical possession of no-man's-land was claimed by many, with aggressive patrolling, raids and observation being the common practice of British battalions. But it was also more often than not a dumping ground for waste materials; in some cases soldiers were

OBSTACLES

From: *Notes for Infantry Officers on Trench Warfare* (1916)

Front trenches and all trenches which may have to be occupied as fire trenches must be protected by an efficient obstacle. Some form of barbed wire entanglement is the most efficient obstacle and is universally used. A wire entanglement must be broad enough not to be easily bridged or quickly cut through, must be under the close fire of the defence, and near enough to be effectively watched at night. The near edge of the entanglement should be about 20yds from the trench, and it should be at least 10yds broad. A height of 2 feet 6in is sufficient, a greater height only increases its liability to damage by our own fire. Good strong wire entanglements, fixed well-driven posts, should be constructed wherever possible.

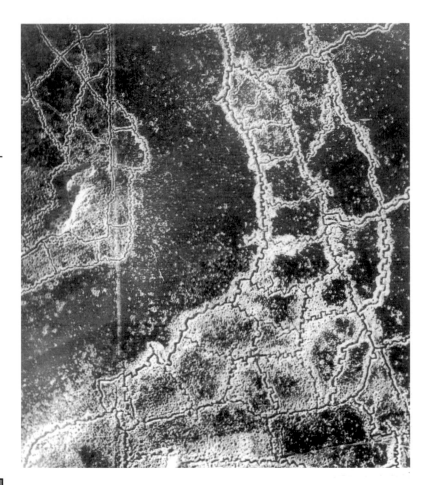

ABOVE The opposing trench lines at Hulluch, showing the trench systems and the presence of no man's land between them.

BELOW The detritus of no-man's-land.

ABOVE Barbed wire obstacles in front of British trenches on the Somme, at Beaumont Hamel.

through trench periscopes set up for the purpose; putting one's head above the trench was virtually suicidal, and head injuries were common in tall soldiers and the curious, especially so before the advent of the steel helmet in 1915–16. By night, sentries were expected to look out over the ground in front of the parapet – a dangerous business when the machine guns were trained at head height to counter this eventuality, and when trenches might only be yards apart.

The forward trenches either side of no-man's-land were protected by belts of barbed wire, an American invention that had seen some limited use in earlier wars, but which was to realise its apogee in the First World War. Barbed wire was to form a significant component of the field defences; but it was to need constant attention. Wiring parties on both sides entered no-man's-land under the cover of darkness: in patrols of two to three men to inspect the integrity of the defences or cut paths through their own wire in preparation for a raid; or, in larger fatigue parties (gangs of anywhere between 12 and 80 men) to repair and improve the front-line wire.

encouraged to fling tins and food containers over the parapet. Although there were obvious concerns over the hygiene of such practice, in many cases it made sense: snipers could hide behind such debris, while would-be attackers might stumble over the waste tins and create a racket, alerting the sentry.

No-man's-land was crossed when soldiers went 'over the top'; when they climbed out over the parapet to face the enemy. For the most part, this ground was observed by day

Wire was brought up the lines by fatigue parties who, usually under the instruction of a sapper officer or NCO, would carry out the work in darkness. Such parties would be in a constant state of readiness; any noise would trigger off a flurry of star shells and Very lights intended to illuminate the interlopers, picking them out in stark silhouette against the night sky, an easy target for a sweeping machine gun or targeted artillery barrage.

The more complex wire constructions involved the hammering in of wooden or angle-iron stakes by a maul; it was not surprising that soldiers feared the attention of the other side. The invention of the screw (or silent) picket – which spread like wildfire on both sides of no-man's-land – meant that complex wire barriers could be constructed relatively noiselessly, soldiers using their entrenching tool helves or other suitable post to wind them into the ground. In a letter home in July 1915, Second Lieutenant A.D. Gillespie describes his discovery of a screw picket: 'We brought in a curious iron stake,

RIGHT Barbed wire obstacles made with screw, or silent pickets, easily screwed into the ground.

which the Germans use for rigging up their barbed wire, made in one piece out of an iron rod looped while the iron is hot, so that the wire can just be threaded through the loops, and it has a corkscrew end, so that it can be screwed into the ground noiselessly.' Reputedly

ABOVE A British wiring party carrying corkscrew wire pickets about to cross the railway line between Arras and Feuchy, May 1917.

manufactured in neutral Sweden and supplied to both sides, the screw picket saw much use during the war.

BARBED-WIRE SCREW PICKETS

The corkscrew picket was made from a round steel bar with its lower section bent into a spiral coil to enable it to be 'screwed' noiselessly into the ground. The 8ft-long picket contained four loops to hold the wire, evenly spaced. The picket was screwed into the ground by turning it in a clockwise direction using as a lever an entrenching tool handle. It was preferable to use the lower loops in order to prevent bending of the picket.

RIGHT AND FAR RIGHT Screw pickets were wound into the ground using the entrenching tool helve; wiring and the repair of obstacles would normally be completed under the cover of darkness.

RIGHT Rolls of barbed wire recovered from the battlefield. British rolls of two-strand wire (top) are distinguished from German rolls of tough, square-section wire (bottom).

BELOW Cutting wire with long-handled wire cutters. Lanes had to be cut in one's own wire to allow the passage of assaulting troops, as well as that of the enemy. It was hoped that the enemy's wire would be sliced by the artillery.

ABOVE British wire cutters: the long handled versions were better suited to cutting the robust German wire.

WIRE CUTTING

The use of barbed-wire cutters was essential in a war where the opposing lines were protected by belts of lethal-looking wire equipped with sharp barbs. While the early cutters were simple in form, and capable of being used by one hand, this did not provide sufficient leverage. The most successful wire-cutting devices were long-handled, with ears capable of guiding the strands into the cutting jaws of the apparatus. Wire cutting was a difficult business, however, as tin cans and other debris designed to make noise were deliberately fitted to entanglements, their purpose to warn of impending assaults.

The wire used by the British and German armies differs to a great extent: British wire is double strand with modest barbs; German wire, tough to work with, is single strand, 2.5mm square-section wire with murderous barbs.

One's own wire was almost as hazardous as that of the enemy, and special paths had to be cut through the tangled maze of wires, lanes that could be targeted by enterprising machine gunners and snipers. To cut the enemy's wire was a hazardous job, as it would be attached to such warning signals as empty tin cans that would clatter alarmingly if approached. Early cutters were largely inadequate; a great variety were tried and patented as the war progressed, and many tested by the Royal Engineers' experimental trench workshops. Makers Chatter Lea made a number of long-handled versions from 1917 that were more satisfactory, but still fraught with difficulties when it came to actual use.

In addition to the variety of hand-held wire cutters, attachments were made for fixing to the muzzle of an infantryman's SMLE that were intended to do the same job. These attachments were ungainly, designed to feed the wire on to jaws that then pivoted when withdrawn, to provide a cut. Given the great tangles encountered by the infantryman in action these cutters were never really a practical proposition in the field. In most cases, cutting the wire was left to the artillery; a skilled business, it required shrapnel to burst at the correct height to obtain the right effect. History shows that this was not always achieved.

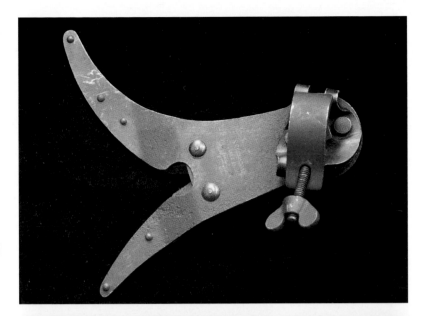

Trench periscopes

Looking over the parapet in daylight was most unwise; snipers would have weapons fixed in position, targeted at dips in the parapet, at latrines and crossing points, and at loophole plates. There was continual loss of life on the Western Front through the actions of snipers in this way, combined with the altogether random attentions of the artillery shell. From early on, the need to be able to look over the parapet to observe activity in no-man's-land led to the production of specially designed 'trench periscopes'.

In an issue of the *Transactions of the Optical Society* for 1915, the basic parameters were laid down for trench periscopes, the object of which, it was stated, was 'to give the soldier a view of his front whilst his head and person are sheltered'. Many patent versions were produced to try and achieve these aims; several of them were adopted officially, others were available for private purchase. For portability, a simple mirror attached to a stick or bayonet was the most effective. Often, such contrivances were more successful than larger box periscopes, which were susceptible to damage from shellfire and which were commonly picked out by snipers. Despite this, day sentries were to be stationed next to a No 9 box periscope, which was in the form of a collapsible and reasonably portable simple wooden box over 25in long, and with a

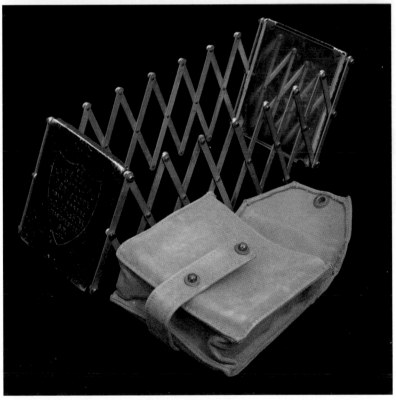

clear field of view sufficient for most trench duties. As the top mirror was vulnerable to sniping, care was taken to protect the observer from glass splinters. Although portable, such periscopes were fixed at sentry posts throughout front-line trenches, effectively disguised from snipers by the use sandbags and sacking.

Officers were drawn to more portable periscopes, and early on in the war, the

ABOVE Duerrs' 'Lifeguard' trench periscope, one of several commercial patterns available to officers.

BOX PERISCOPE

A sentry positions a box periscope. Simply constructed the box shape was often easily identified by snipers, who would also look for reflections off the mirror glass to aim at. Spare glass was provided with the No 9 periscope for this reason, and there was a shutter that could be closed part-way so that the observer's eyes were protected from the fall of shards of broken glass. The periscope was fixed to the trench slope by a metal bar that could be inserted into its side, holding the instrument fairly steady. During daytime, sentries would not be able to put their head above the parapet for fear of being killed by a sniper's bullet. The periscope, now fixed, gave the sentry a reasonable field of view, sufficient at least to warn of impending attack, or to detect any movement or unusual activity in no-man's-land.

RIGHT Fitting and observing no-man's-land through the No 9 Box Periscope.

'Lifeguard' trench periscope, manufactured and patented by the Manchester firm of F. Duerrs was widely advertised in the press. This periscope was constructed on the expanding 'lazy tong' principle, which when extended provided the required two opposed mirrors separated by 2ft; when collapsed the device was only 2in deep. The commonest periscope used by officers was the Beck's No 25, issued from 1917, which comprised a simple small-diameter brass tube, with detachable handle and a focusing eyepiece. This effective piece of equipment was not only light, durable and difficult to spot at a distance, and long enough to provide the observer sufficient protection, it was also a magnifying periscope.

Trench routine

From the advent of trench warfare in late 1914, there emerged a routine that would come to encompass the world of the average soldier, one that would provide some order to an otherwise bizarre experience of living in a ditch, during which time the normal civilised code of activity in the day and rest at night would become reversed. Battalions coming into the line to relieve the garrison had to maintain a routine that would ensure that the transition was smooth, and that the officers were in a position to take over command. The activities essential to relieving the trenches were described in Lake's *Knowledge for War. Every Officer's Handbook for the Front*.

By day, sentries were posted at box periscopes or their simple mirror equivalents, one per platoon, looking out for *minenwerfers*, gas and unusual activity. By night, sentries would stand nervously on the fire step, anticipating the casual and random play of a machine gun across no-man's-land. Between times, there would be inspections, trench repair and the issue of rations, brought up by ration carriers from the rear areas.

The trenches at night were a hive of activity, and sentries had to maintain a high level of alertness, even though their lack of sleep during the day would tempt them to nap – a military crime of a most serious nature. The cloying darkness magnified the noises that emanated from no-man's-land. As such, this barren strip

IN THE TRENCHES

From: *Knowledge for War. Every Officer's Handbook for the Front* (1916)

1 Preparatory to entering.
Check periscopes, water bottles, glasses, water-carriers, stretchers, field-dressings, emergency rations, smoke helmets, rifle accessories, identity discs, sandbags, ammunition. Water bottles to be filled. Magazines to be charged and bayonets fixed and unfixed beforehand, to ensure proper working.

2 Taking over trenches.
Ascertain position of officers' dugouts. Arrange telephones, see and check stores and tools, carefully note reserve ammunition. Obtain rough sketch of front and number of traverses to be manned. See that wire entanglements in front of trenches are absolutely intact. Arrange for water and find out position of latrines.

3 On arrival.
Post sentries, arrange visiting rounds, check and explain gas alarms, arrange for ammunition.

4 Routine.
Each sentry to have a periscope, and to be on watch for one hour only. Whole company to stand to arms at dusk and one hour before dawn. Bombs to be kept under cover. All men to know position of latrines and water supply. Each platoon to have its own ammunition reserve, and all men to know where this is. Rifles should be inspected twice daily. Loopholes should be inspected at dusk. Drains should be watched, and every effort made to keep trenches dry.

of land was regularly lit up brilliantly by flares, star shells fired by artillery, coloured warning rockets launched from the front line, and smaller Very (or Verey) lights, the term originating from their American inventor, Edward W. Very. These flares were usually fired by officers from hand-

held pistols, which threw up 'light balls' into the dark night sky.

Working parties were also to move forward into the contested zone at night, to make repairs, carry out patrols and investigate suspicious objects. They had to be ever vigilant – star shells and Very lights would cause working parties to be starkly silhouetted against the skyline; warning rockets were fired to alert the artillery in case of attack. Opportunistic bursts of fixed machine guns were a threat, as were nervous sentries on one's own side.

For both allies and foe, trench routine usually commenced with 'stand-to' (from 'stand to arms') at one hour before dawn, when all troops

in the front line would position themselves on the fire step armed and ready to confront an attacker – the theory being that most attacks would take place at dawn. 'Stand-to' would last at least an hour –and –a half, but would finish when the enemy parapet could be seen through the periscopes set up along the line of the trenches. It was invariably accompanied by a fusillade of bullets fired off into the unknown space of no-man's-land. Often called the 'mad minute' or 'wind up', men would blast away to make their enemies aware of their existence.

This activity would soon die away, duty done, and peace resumed on both sides. Following 'stand-to', most men were stood down, but left sentries on duty, one per platoon, to man the fixed box periscopes. A tot of rum would then be issued to each man, a welcome respite from the often freezing conditions. Rum was issued at dawn and dusk, following 'Stand-to'. The issue of a rum ration in the armed forces was a British institution – though it was frowned upon by some commanders.

Service rum was thick and robust; its positive effects after a night on the fire step are remembered in most soldiers' memoirs. Rum was issued from ceramic jugs labelled 'SRD'. These initials have spawned a host of jokey explanations, from 'Soon Runs Dry' to 'Seldom Reaches Destination'. Rather more prosaic, the initials stood for 'Supply Reserve Depot', a large establishment based in Deptford, repository of many such stores. Famously, rum was also issued to those men about to go 'over the bags', either at dawn with a large-scale attack, or at night prior to a raid. The ration was issued by a senior NCO, under close inspection of an officer, the fiery effect of this viscous liquid being a boon in the cold, damp conditions of the trench.

Given that drunkenness was a serious offence, the ration could not be accumulated and saved for later; poured into mug or mess tin top it was to be drunk in the presence of the officer. It was a long-held tradition that, like the issue of strawberry jam, any rum residue left in a jug was taken by the sergeant – a perk of his position. Soldiers were otherwise not entitled to alcohol in the trenches – although officers' messes were to receive such precious liquids from home.

Breakfast followed, with the meal comprising rations that had been brought up at night and were meant to last for a 48-hour period. Tea, bacon, bread – these were the staples of trench food, but often it could be simply bully beef and biscuits. Food was a difficult issue for High Command: tinned food was relatively plentiful, but 'bully beef' – ration corned beef – was hardly warming in the cold of Flanders, and was not well received by the soldiers themselves.

To relieve the monotony, and give sustenance to the men in the front line, ration parties would bring up provisions at night, usually men 'out at rest' detailed for work up the line who returned to their rest camps at night. With increasing sophistication of the military machine, hot rations in specially designed carriers were brought up the line; negotiating long communication trenches in the dark meant that this was often an arduous duty, but one much appreciated by the front-line troops all the same.

All other rations would be brought up in sandbags, often in a hopeless jumble of loose tea, sugar, bread, bacon and tins, intended for a period of 48 hours. Corned beef – 'bully' to the troops – was imported, then as now, from South America, and was variously received. Other tinned food staples included 'pork and beans' – tinned beans with a small cube of pork fat at the bottom of the tin – and the universal Maconochie ration – a tinned vegetable and meat concoction akin to Irish stew that at least

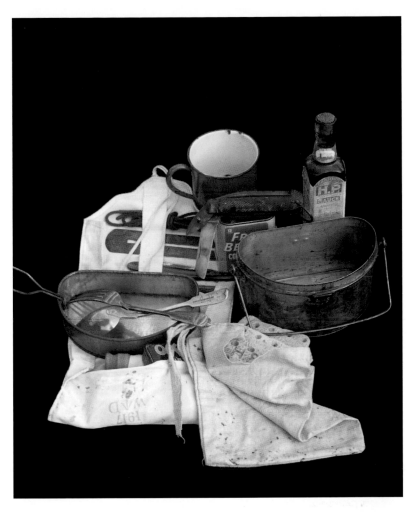

ABOVE **Mess tins, basic rations and sauces to make them more palatable.**

BELOW **Canadian soldiers have a meal of bully and bread in the trenches. The rum jar is likely to contain water.**

served to break the monotony of bully beef. Jam – 'pozzy' in soldiers' slang – was another welcome ration, although the frequency with which 'plum and apple' flavours were issued left a lot to be desired. Fresh rations, such as meat, bacon and vegetables, would also be supplied, brought to the front in the ubiquitous sandbag.

Braziers – buckets with holes punched in them – would be a means of keeping warm, as well as cooking, but their glow could be seen for some distance. Cooking in the trenches required some nerve. Too much smoke and the enemy guns could rain down a fusillade of 'whizz-bangs' – high-velocity shells – or send over 'minnies', the much feared *minenwerfer* trench mortars, capable of destroying sections of trenches, and their occupants. Small fires were used for frying bacon, heating Maconochie rations or brewing tea; braver souls in quieter sectors used braziers fuelled with issues of coke or more often pieces of broken trench boards. An 'old sweat's' approach was the use of a candle stub, cigarette tin and 'four be' two' flannel, to boil water, slowly, enough for a mug of hot 'char'. Most coveted was the paraffin-fuelled Primus pressure stove, a sophisticated and efficient piece of engineering invented in the late 19th century – a rare luxury in the trenches.

For the soldier in the front line, water was supplied in petrol tins, carried to the front with ration parties. As Shell Oil was the main supplier of fuel to the British army, Shell petrol tins were undoubtedly seen in the front line as water carriers. Unfortunately, the water would never quite lose its petrol taste – something even the strongest tea could not defeat. Rum jars were also used for water when empty, presumably with a more palatable undertaste. Mineral waters and sodas sent from home – Schweppes bottles were common in the trenches – also provided some respite from the usual petrol-tainted water.

After breakfast, it was time for platoon commanders to make their inspection of rifles. Cleaning rifles in the muddy conditions during the winter months, or even when the mud had dried to dust in the summer months, was a major challenge to all men in the trenches. Officers' attention was focused on breech and chamber, parts of the gun liable to fouling from mud and dirt, a significant issue in the miry trenches of the Ypres salient.

CARE OF RIFLES IN THE TRENCHES

From: *Knowledge for War. Every Officer's Handbook for the Front* (1916)

Rifles should be inspected every morning in the trenches by the platoon commander, and at other times during the day by the sergeant or section commanders. It should be impressed on men that ammunition must be kept clean, or rifles are apt to jamb.

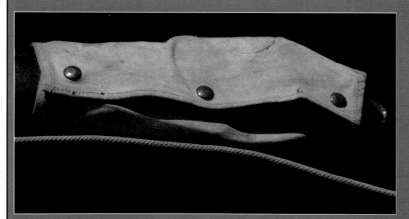

ABOVE Breech covers, or simply sandbags, were used to keep the action clean and free from fouling.

Principal defects:

A Mud in bolt, owing to the rifle being rested on wet parapet, or dropped on wet ground. REMEDY: Cover bolt when not in use with canvas cover or with old sock.

B Muddy ammunition resulting in mud in chamber. REMEDY: Prohibit placing of ammunition on ground and provide proper boxes for it.

C Mud in muzzle resulting from rifles being pushed into sides of trenches. REMEDY: Careful and frequent inspection. Rifles must be clean before firing.

D Sticking of cartridges owing to dirt in chamber and magazine.

E Rust in lock and insufficient oiling. REMEDY: Bolt and magazine must be tested daily. Cartridges never to be kept in chamber.

With rifles cleaned and inspected, and the men fed, those soldiers not on 'sentry-go' were detailed for fatigues to repair trenches and engage in similar activities. These pursuits would go on throughout the day, only broken for lunch at midday – drawing on the rations brought up to the front line – and an evening meal at around 6pm. No soldiers in their right minds would place themselves at risk by moving around the front line in the daytime, and reminders (in the form of signboards) of trenches requiring repair, and dangerous corners, were strategically placed in order to save soldiers' lives from snipers and from those taking random potshots. Soldiers had to be vigilant at all times.

Night routine would commence with another 'stand-to' before dusk, and another officers' inspection. The trenches then came alive to a custom of repair, supply and patrol, with men engaged on endless trench improvement, and with patrols and wiring parties out in no-man's-land, keeping an eye open for star shells that could catch them starkly silhouetted against the sky, targets for watchful sentries and searching machine guns. Night sentries, with a round in the chamber ready for an alert, were detailed to look over the parapet – dangerous when the enemy had his guns trained at head height for the same reason.

Sleeping on sentry duty was a capital offence; experienced NCOs made it their business to visit their charges every 15 minutes, and officers would also be vigilant in their duties. Other men would be allowed to sleep, if they were lucky, or be detailed to go on endless carrying details, bringing up supplies from the rear along communication trenches, a truly prodigious effort in the often-congested earthworks.

With these fortifications under continuous, random bombardment, trench boards, duckboards and revetments needed constant upkeep. With men 'out on rest' bringing supplies to the reserve trenches, more often than not it would be the front-line troops who would have to ensure they were delivered to their destinations, and who would have to work to improve the lot of the trenches, or to go out under the cover of darkness to repair the wire. Carrying such material, even in the best of conditions, was back-breaking work; even more so if the landscape was churned up by war.

LEFT A sentry of the 12th East Yorkshires on the firestep of a snow-covered trench keeps watch over no-man's-land.

1908 WEB INFANTRY EQUIPMENT: 'BATTLE ORDER'

Information from: *The Pattern 1908 Web Infantry Equipment* (1913)

'Battle order' represented the equipment of the soldier in the trenches. It was mandatory for men to wear their equipment at all times. The soldier also wore his steel helmet.

1 *Front view*
Fully loaded, the cartridge carriers contain 150 rounds of .303 ball ammunition. Each carrier has five pouches capable of carrying three chargers of five rounds each. The set is adjusted to fit comfortably.

2 *Right view*
The haversack is in position attached to the brace straps, the water bottle in its carrier is suspended from the end of the brace straps (right) and the equivalent strap at the rear of the belt (left).

3 *Rear view*
The haversack is attached to the brace straps, in place of the pack, using the two additional buckles locked into position using equivalent tabs on the rear of the haversack. The haversack contains the soldier's 'necessaries' and rations etc. Here the entrenching tool is carried at the rear, suspended from the brace straps; the haversack, bayonet and entrenching tool helve are carried on the left of the soldier. Suspended from the rear of the haversack (using the straps and buckles of the pack) are the mess tin and the cotton bag containing the soldier's 'unexpired rations'.

4 *Left view*
The bayonet and attached entrenching tool helve is readily accessible; the helve cleverly attaches to the bayonet by an additional web strap.

1914-PATTERN INFANTRY EQUIPMENT: 'BATTLE ORDER'

Information from: *The Pattern 1914 Leather Infantry Equipment* (1915)

The soldier wears his steel helmet, with sacking cover used to disguise its distinctive silhouette.

1 *Front view*
Fully loaded, the cartridge carriers contain 60 rounds of .303 ball ammunition. Each carrier has the capacity to take a cotton bandolier, each bandolier comprising five cotton pouches with two chargers of five bullets in each.

2 *Right view*
The pack is in position attached to the brace straps, the water bottle in its carrier suspended from the end of the brace straps (right) and the equivalent strap at the rear of the belt (left).

3 *Rear view*
The haversack, in webbing with leather straps, is fastened to the brace straps using two additional tongued buckles, which are locked into position using leather tabs with holes that are to the rear of the pack. The leather entrenching tool holder is suspended from leather straps.

4 *Left view*
The bayonet and the entrenching tool helve are readily accessible.

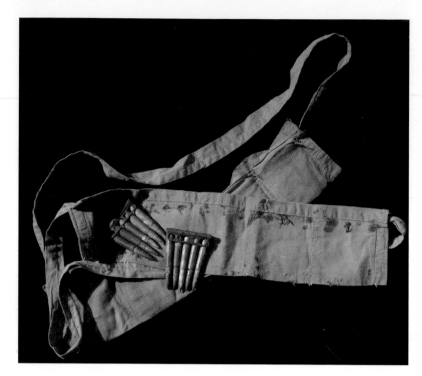

ABOVE Cotton bandoliers carried five chargers of .303 ammunition.

It was mandatory that web equipment be worn in the trenches; it could only be removed, temporarily, when visiting the latrine. Despite this, it was rare indeed that the full equipment set would be worn; instead, the large pack (containing greatcoat and a range of other items) would be sent back with the battalion transport. The full equipment set was known as 'marching order'; when in the front line, the

RIGHT A soldier prepares to carry ammunition up to the trenches. Though shouldering a box of grenades, carrying a box of ammunition would be a lot more difficult.

small pack would be transferred to the back, redistributing the weight of the set, in what became known as 'battle order'.

'Battle order' was also used for the emergency 1914-pattern leather equipment.

Nevertheless, trenches were also modified so that men could reach their equipment more efficiently – and particularly access to ammunition. In the front line, soldiers had to carry 150 rounds of small-arms ammunition (SAA) in their pouches, forming their reserve – and their primary source of ammunition when in action. The standard bullet was the .303in-calibre Mark VII infantry bullet (pointed and thus distinguished from the older Mark VI which was used by the navy and Territorial battalions still using the long Lee-Enfield-pattern rifle). Issued in cotton bandoliers holding five chargers of five rounds each, these bandoliers were packed in ammunition boxes, an open box of which was kept in each fire bay (although the authorities frowned upon the draping of bandoliers from appropriate points in the trenches as being untidy).

On average, men spent a period of four to eight days in the front line, but this depended very much on circumstances, with some battalions employed longer in hard-pressed areas. Private Herbert Mason of the 6th Battalion, Oxfordshire and Buckinghamshire Light Infantry clandestinely recorded his trench duties while serving in the 20th (Light) Division at Ypres. In 1915–16, his tours of the trenches lasted between four and eleven days in the salient, and this is typical for many. While some men were in the front fire trenches, others would occupy the support lines behind, ready to provide reinforcement when hard pressed in an attack or raid. There was to be a rhythm to trench warfare, with typically five days in the front line, five in reserve, five at the front again and finally five days in reserve. Relief when it came saw the battalion removed from the front-line trenches and taken to the rear areas, where they would be billeted in farm buildings, and where they could receive both pay and the ability to buy such comforts as *oeuf-frites*, *café au lait*, and beer. During this period, reinforcements and replacements for losses sustained would arrive, and men would be trained in the use of new weapons, gas procedures and other aspects of the evolving war.

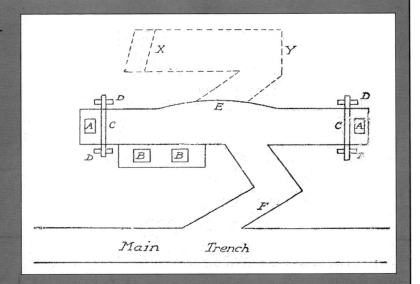

ABOVE Latrines were commonly the target of attention for enemy artillery fire.

Trench hygiene

Maintaining strict standards of hygiene in the trenches was difficult, particularly where casualties lay out in no-man's-land, encouraging rats, flies and other vermin. Tommy was expected to maintain military standards of cleanliness wherever possible, although in winter this was often challenging. Orders specified the collection and adequate disposal of rubbish, but some tins were deliberately pitched over the parapet to act as early warning signals as men approaching the wire tripped over or kicked them. In some cases, sandbags were provided for rubbish, while others were hung from trench sides for the collection of spent cartridges and chargers.

Latrines were supplied as small trenches off the supervision trench in the front line, and it was the duty of the 'sanitary man' to empty these buckets – he, in turn, was not generally expected to go over the top with the rest of his company.

Lice were the constant companion of the soldier in the trenches, the inevitable consequence of gathering large groups of men without the ability to change their clothes regularly. Gathered into the warmth of the seams of the woollen uniforms, and clustered in the intimate parts of the soldiers' bodies, lice multiplied rapidly and spread from man to man. The adult body louse (*Pediculus vestimenti* in Latin), with a lifespan of around four weeks, lived by clinging to the undergarments, close enough to the skin in order to feed, while still attached to the cloth. Their frequent desire to feed caused great discomfort, sores and, eventually, infections. Tommy would resort to removal of the 'chats' by hand, running the

BELOW Men of the 15th Royal Welch Fusiliers (London Welsh) filling sandbags with the earth excavated in the construction of a dug-out in their trenches at Fleurbaix, December 1917.

THE LOUSE

From: *The Minor Horrors of War* (1915)

The habitat of the body-louse is that side of the under-clothing which is in contact with the body. The louse, which sucks the blood of its host at least twice a day, is when feeding always anchored to the inside of the underclothing of its host by the claws of one or more of its six legs. In times of war, when men are aggregated in large numbers and personal cleanliness – but especially an adequate change of clothing – cannot be secured, infestation with lice commonly takes place. To avoid these pests the following rules should be observed:

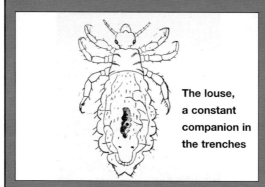

The louse, a constant companion in the trenches

A Search your personas often as possible for signs of the presence of lice.
B Try not to sleep where others, especially the unclean, have slept before.
C Change your clothing as often as practicable. After clothes have been discarded for a week the lice are usually dead from starvation. Jolting of kit in transport aids in spreading the lice, which become disseminated by crawling about from one kit to another.
D Verminous clothes for which there is not further use should be burnt, buried or sunk in water.
E Underclothes may be scalded. Turn coats, trousers, etc, inside out, examine beneath the folds at the seams and expose these places to as much heat as can be borne before a fire. Petrol or paraffin will also kill lice in clothing. If no other means are available, turn the clothing inside out, beat it vigorously, remove and kill the vermin by hand – this will, at any rate, mitigate the evil.

fingernail through seams or playing a candle flame along them, and hearing the insects 'pop' (but thereby weakening uniforms). Commercial powders – such as Keating's – were considered to be practically useless by soldiers, who soundly believed it to encourage the vermin to multiply. Nonetheless, such treatments were sent regularly from home.

Trench fever was a viral disease usually classified at the time as 'pyrexia of unknown origin'. With men suffering extreme fevers with high temperatures and all that goes with such symptoms, those with 'trench fever' were often hospitalised. Unidentified at the time, a link was made post-war with the bites of body lice, the inevitable consequence of confining so many men in difficult conditions. So lice were considered a severe health risk.

While lice contributed to the discomfort of the trenches, the cold and wet conditions suffered by most men made life in the trenches – in winter at least – an almost unbearable experience. The damp soon told on the men's well-being, and in particular the condition known as trench feet. 'Trench feet' was caused by prolonged immersion of the feet in water; it required a significant commitment to its prevention if men were not to be eventually hospitalised. The constant soaking meant that the outer skin of men's feet became sore and then deadened to sensation, exacerbated by restrictive boots and over-tight puttees that interrupted circulation. Eventually, the condition could lead to decay and ultimately gangrene – with amputation the only solution. The army was understandably concerned over this debilitating complaint, and in the absence of trench waders or other forms of rubber boots, constant care of the feet, including inspections, manipulation with whale oil, and frequent changes of socks were constantly advertised to the rank and file.

CARE OF FEET

From: *Knowledge for War. Every Officer's Handbook for the Front* (1916)

Care of the feet in trenches was deemed to be of the utmost importance, and officers were instructed to maintain constant vigilance over their men. The *Handbook* recognised the need for attention to detail in caring for feet and combatting 'frostbite and chilled feet'.

CAUSE:

A Prolonged standing in cold water or liquid mud.

B Tight boots and puttees, which interfere with the circulation.

PRECAUTIONS:

A Before going into trenches the feet and legs to be washed and dried; then rubbed with whale oil or anti-freeze mixture, and dry socks put on. A second pair of dry socks to be carried.

B Boots and socks to be taken off from time to time when in the trenches, and the feet washed and dried and rubbed again with fat.

C Hot water not to be used, nor feet held near a fire.

D Men must wear gum boots served out, only in the trenches. On no account must they be allowed to wear them when in billets or in localities a considerable distance behind the trenches.

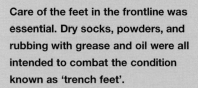

Care of the feet in the frontline was essential. Dry socks, powders, and rubbing with grease and oil were all intended to combat the condition known as 'trench feet'.

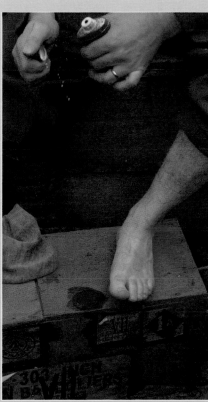

Chapter Four

Trench warfare

Trench warfare began in earnest on the Western Front in November 1914, when the manoeuvring armies dug in to prevent being outflanked. With the war stalemated into a long siege dominated by machine guns and artillery, other weapons were developed to try and break it – grenades and gas, and trench raids saw a reversion to knives and clubs.

OPPOSITE The debris of battle: shellholes and barbed wire pickets in no-man's-land.

16. BRITISH MACHINE GUNNERS WEARING GAS HELMETS
OFFICIAL PHOTOGRAPH. CROWN COPYRIGHT RESERVED

ABOVE A classic image of war. British machine gunners operate a Vickers .303 whilst wearing PH Gas Helmets. (Note they have their issue spoons tucked into their puttees.)

The First World War is closely associated with the development of weapons designed to inflict the maximum loss of life on the protagonists. Of these weapons, it is perhaps the machine guns that are associated by most with the reign of death on the battlefield, and effective they were in scything through the attacking formations, so much so that gallantry medals were often awarded for the capture or destruction of machine-gun posts; it is not surprising that the armies were at pains to disguise them.

Despite the power of the machine gun, it was probably artillery fire that was most feared, its devastating effects evident in the destruction of the landscape, and in the often random death caused by the explosion of shells of all calibres, the frailness of the human body being all too apparent. Artillery fire became increasingly sophisticated as the war progressed, with timed barrages designed to 'lift', maintaining a rolling effect in front of an advance, or the isolation of raiding parties in box barrages, deterring the enemy from attacking by walls of shells. Trench maps and other innovations were a function of the need to

accurately place shellfire, and a complex system of grid coordinates was evolved to achieve this. The gunners were constant companions in arms to the infantry, providing barrage fire at the opening of offensives, and frequently called upon – through signal flares and fragile telephone lines – to deal with troublesome machine-gun nests, snipers and suspicious activity in no-man's-land.

Machine guns

The British army went to war with the machine gun as a specialist weapon, with two heavy Vickers (or Maxim) machine guns per infantry battalion. The Vickers .303 had been introduced in 1912 as a replacement for the earlier Maxim Mark I, which had been the first machine gun in British service, from 1889. The Maxim gun was a water-cooled, belt-fed machine gun, the belt made from cloth or tarpaulin. It was fired using a toggle lock action that had been invented by Hiram Maxim himself. The Vickers was an advance on the earlier gun, although it used basically the same action as its predecessor, albeit improvements (and use of steel for brass parts) meant that the gun was 20lb lighter than the Maxim, at 40lb, excluding the water used for cooling and the weighty tripod. While the Vickers machine gun became famous, and was to see service long after the war had ended, existing Maxims were also used.

The general characteristics of the Vickers were described in the company brochure:

1. The gun is fully automatic in action, the force of recoil of the barrel (when a cartridge is fired) being used to actuate the loading and firing mechanism;
2. The ammunition is fed into the gun through the use of non-distintegrating canvas belts with a capacity of 250 rounds of .303 ammunition;
3. Ammunition belts consist of two strips of canvas bound together by brass strips to form pockets to hold the cartridges, brass tags at the end of the belt facilitate loading;
4. The barrel is water-cooled, enabling the gun to be fired for long periods without becoming overheated;

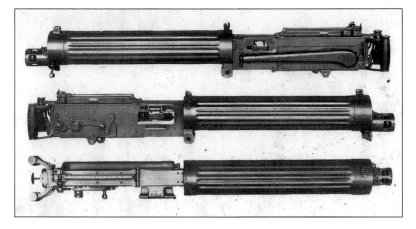

5. The mechanism is robust, and able to withstand prolonged firing;
6. The mechanism is readily accessible, and both the feed and lock components are self-contained, such that they can be readily removed or replaced;
7. The gun will not fire until the breech is closed; and
8. The gun can be fired at all angles of elevation or depression, without adjustment of the mechanism itself.

ABOVE The Vickers machine gun, from the Vickers' Company guide.

BELOW The Vickers machine gun, showing the deployment of the tripod, with the position of the auxiliary tripod.

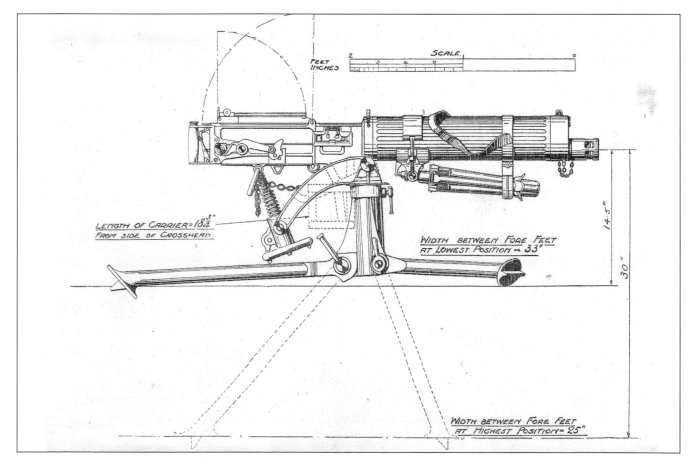

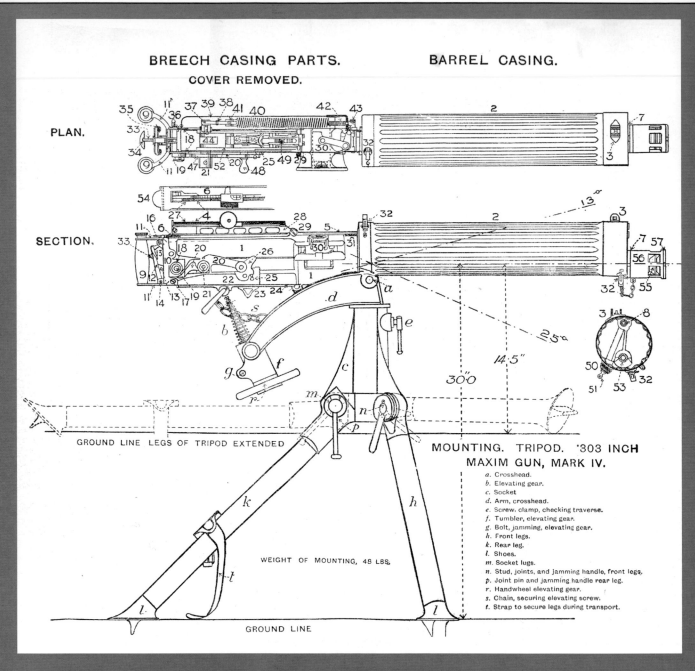

BREECH CASING PARTS.   BARREL CASING.
COVER REMOVED.

PLAN.

SECTION.

GROUND LINE LEGS OF TRIPOD EXTENDED

MOUNTING. TRIPOD. '303 INCH
MAXIM GUN, MARK IV.

a. Crosshead.
b. Elevating gear.
c. Socket.
d. Arm, crosshead.
e. Screw, clamp, checking traverse.
f. Tumbler, elevating gear.
g. Bolt, jamming, elevating gear.
h. Front legs.
k. Rear leg.
l. Shoes.
m. Socket lugs.
n. Stud, joints, and jamming handle, front legs.
p. Joint pin and jamming handle rear leg.
r. Handwheel elevating gear.
s. Chain, securing elevating screw.
t. Strap to secure legs during transport.

WEIGHT OF MOUNTING, 48 LBS.

GROUND LINE

The Vickers .303 machine gun showing its component parts

1 Casing, breech.	14 Pin, screwed, axis, safety catch.	24 Plate, bottom, breech casing.	36 Pin-T, fixing, rear-crosspiece.	47 Tail of crank handle.
2 Casing, barrel.	15 (not used).	25 Bracket, check lever.	37 Fusee.	48 Knob of crank handle.
3 Bracket, fore-sight.	16 Pin, screwed, axis, safety catch.	26 Lever, check.	38 Chain, fusee.	49 Casing, lock.
4 Sight, tangent.	17 Pin, screwed, joint, rear- crosspiece.	27 Base of tangent sight stem.	39 Box, fusee spring.	50 Protector, screwed, condenser. boss.
5 Cover, front.	18 Slides, right and left.	28 Bridge, rear cover.	40 Spring, fusee.	51 Plug, cork.
6 Cover, rear.	19 Roller.	29 Pin, screwed, joint cover.	41 Hook, fusee spring.	52 Plate, side, right.
7 Gland.	20 Handle, crank.	30 Block, feed.	42 Screw, adjusting, fusee spring.	53 Barrel.
8 Tube, steam.	21 Pin, screwed, fixing, crank handle.	31 Catch, front cover.	43 Lever of catch, front cover.	54 Lock, rear cover.
9 Grips, rear-crosspiece.	22 Bracket, elevating joint.	32 Plug, screwed.	44 Crank.	55 Cup, muzzle attachment.
10 Rear-crosspiece.	23 Stop, mounting.	33 Thumbpiece, firing lever.	45 Rod, connecting.	56 Casing, outer, muzzle attachment.
11 Arms of rear-crosspiece.		34 Ditto.	46 Socket of side levers for 53.	57 Cone, front, muzzle attachment.
12 Lever, firing.		35 Finger grips, safety catch.		
13 Pawl, firing lever.				

The Vickers and Maxim machine guns were complex but robust, as they had to be to stand up to military service. The Vickers Company provided a bewildering list of parts with technical terms to allow specific ordering of replacements by the War Office; the average machine gunner also needed to be highly trained and proficient in handling the gun itself. Similar lists were issued by a number of commercial publications, such as the *Guide for the .303 Vickers Machine Gun*, published in 1915.

As no one had expected the war to be a static one – with an increased role for the machine gun in both defensive (protecting a position) and offensive (creating a barrage) – this was hardly surprising. Machine gunners were to become an elite arm. The power of the British Vickers Mark I machine gun and its German

MG08 Maxim equivalent, was truly frightening. Fired in short bursts of 200 rounds per minute (although both had a rate of fire of 450 rounds per minute) both guns had a maximum effective range of 2,000yds, accuracy and hit rate increasing as the range decreased.

Preparing the machine gun for firing depended on the following procedure, as set out in the Vickers Company handbook for the weapon:

1 Pass the tag end of the belt through the feed block from the right-hand side.
2 Turning the crank handle to the rear will withdraw the lock from the barrel and wind the fusee links to extend the fusee spring.
3 Pulling the belt to the left as far as it will go brings a cartridge into the centre of the feed block, where it is then retained by the pawls.

ABOVE Vickers gun team.

4 When the crank handle is released, the lock will be propelled forwards by the unwinding of the fusee links by the fusee spring. The extractor will then engage the cartridge in the feed block.

5 Turning the crank handle for a second time will withdraw the cartridge from the feed block by the extractor, placing it in line with the barrel.

6 Pulling the belt to the left again will bring a second cartridge into the centre of the feed block.

7 Releasing the crank handle means that the lock will move forward to engage the first cartridge in the barrel, and the extractor will also engage the second cartridge in the feed block.

Following this procedure, the gun was ready to fire. Firing it involved:

1. Raising the trigger safety catch and pressing the trigger. The act of pressing the trigger

ABOVE AND LEFT Mounting and preparing the .303 Vickers machine gun.

BELOW LEFT AND RIGHT Dismounting the machine gun to be fired using the auxiliary tripod.

is transmitted to the handsear in the lock through the trigger pawl, the trigger lever and the trigger bar.

2. With the handsear activated, its lower portion is brought out of engagement with the bent on the tumbler. This is then free to pivot on its axis pin, permitting the firing pin to be propelled forwards under the action of the main spring, thereby firing the cartridge.

On recoil of the gun, the action prepares it to fire the next cartridge. This involved:

1 The extractor gripping the second cartridge in the feed block, while the empty cartridge will be in the barrel chamber.

2 The recoil of the barrel and other parts some 25mm extends the fusee spring. The tail of the crank handle then engages with the roller to force the handle and the crank to rotate, thereby withdrawing the lock from the barrel. The fusee is also rotated, winding the fusee links, and putting additional tension on the fusee spring.

3 With the lock moving backwards, the extractor withdraws the live cartridge from the feed block, and the empty case from the barrel. The path of the extractor is guided by the side cams and rear cover extractor guides, and engages with the horns of the extractor to deflect it downwards when the live cartridge has been withdrawn from the feed block. The live cartridge is placed in line with the barrel, and the empty case drops from the extractor.

The action of the recoil also repositioned the firing pin and the next cartridge in the belt. The cycle of operations continued as long as the trigger was pressed – and there was sufficient water in the jacket to ensure that the barrel remained cooled, and therefore less likely to jam.

According to the War Office manual, *Infantry Training, 1914*, machine guns like the Vickers operated on a frontage of 2yds, from which it could deliver a volume of fire that was equal to the effects of 30 men firing rapidly; even then frontage required to match the effects would be some 15 times as great. It was also calculated that even if the volume of fire could be matched by infantrymen, the effects of firing a machine

gun were still twice as much. Given these facts, taken together with the knowledge that the Vickers could theoretically fire indefinitely (so long as it was cooled by a plentiful supply of water, and had enough ammunition), it is not surprising that the number of machine guns in service escalated as the war progressed. The deployment of these weapons and the development of tactics became more complex as trench warfare became stalemated. With each weapon came a crew of at least three men: the No 1, responsible for firing and upkeep, but carrying the tripod; No 2, in charge of loading, as well as carrying the weapon itself, and the No 3, accountable for the wider supply

Points to note :— **Normal Firing Position (Sitting).**
1. Gun and Tripod mounted correctly at suitable height, with belt box in position.
2. Condenser tube passed through the loop of front carrying handle.
3. Condenser bag screened as far as possible.
4. *No. 1.*—Feet closed in and firmly planted in ground.
5. Correct method of taking " holding " pressure with both hands.
6. Elbows supported inside the thighs. 7. Eyes directed towards the target.
8. *No. 2.*—Lowest possible position. 9. Right hand assisting feed belt.
10. Observing controlling officer from position below the gun.
11. Left hand out horizontally indicating " Ready to fire."

ABOVE The normal position for firing the Vickers whilst sitting.

BELOW Firing the Vickers using the auxiliary tripod.

Firing with Auxiliary Tripod.

Points to note :—
1. Feet of tripod forced in ground by No. 2.
2. Sights upright.
3. *No. 1.*—Correct " holding " with both hands.
4. Elbows splayed out to support gun and body.
5. *No. 2.*—Assisting feed belt with right hand.
6. Left hand out indicating " Gun ready to fire."
7. Watching controlling officer.

RIGHT Lewis gun
in action, fired by a
Gurkha soldier 'in the
trenches'.

BELOW The Lewis
gun, from the *Machine
Gunners Handbook*,
1917. Parts: 7. Butt
Latch. 26. Receiver. 30.
Trigger. 38. Charging
Handle. 39. Guard. 61.
Gear Casing. 65. Gear
Case Hinge Pin. 68.
Receiver Lock Pin. 81.
Gas Regulator Key. 84.
Gas Regulator Cup. 88.
Clamp Ring Screw.

of the weapon. Carrying no rifles, all three were vulnerable, so were equipped with the Webley Mark VI revolver for personal protection.

Infantry Training, 1914 also recognised the value of the Vickers in the defence of cramped localities, such as salients and defended villages, as well as in laying down powerful 'enfilade' fire along a set feature, such as a wall, or trench. With concentrated firepower available rapidly, it was superb in defence, excellent both in covering the advance of infantry and in repelling attacks, and capable of traversing rapidly. There were weaknesses, however. The Vickers was large, its crew of three needed if the weapon was to be redeployed, and under surprise attack it was vulnerable to being overtaken and captured. But these limitations in no way undermined the merit of the weapons in trench warfare.

With deeper considerations of machine-gun tactics, came the idea in 1915 that the Vickers guns should be taken away from infantry battalions and given, in larger numbers, to the newly formed Machine Gun Corps (MGC). In this way, the role of MGC was guided from the divisional commanders, in order that it might provide effective infantry support. In

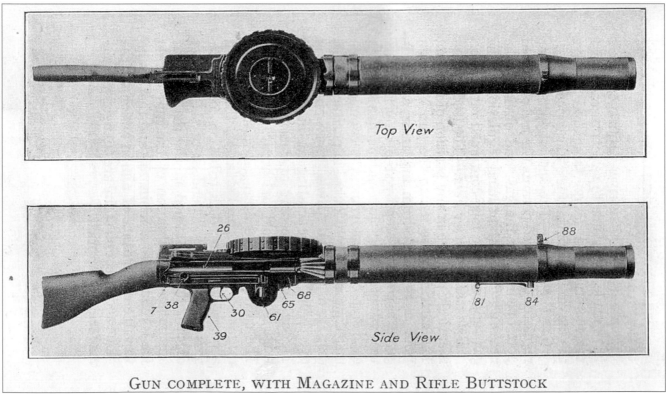

Top View

Side View

GUN COMPLETE, WITH MAGAZINE AND RIFLE BUTTSTOCK

return for their loss, infantry battalions were issued with the lighter Lewis gun, a hand-held weapon that was more suited to an infantry role. The manual *Infantry Machine Gun Training 1917* compared the characteristics of the two weapons. Whereas the Vickers could sustain fire for some time, the Lewis, cooled only by air and supplied with limited ammunition in drums, could not. The heavier machine gun was also capable of being mounted in a position that would guarantee an accurate direction of fire; the Lewis, not fitted with a tripod, was designed to be fired from the shoulder in the manner of a rifle. This in turn enabled the Lewis to be deployed quickly, and on the move.

The Lewis light machine gun was of American design, but was to see its most widespread use in British service. The weapon was gas operated, and air cooled; in infantry service its barrel was fitted with an aluminium jacket with vanes that acted as a radiator. Protected by a large tubular sleeve that was open at both ends, the act of firing the gun created an airflow over the vanes, thereby cooling the weapon. The basic action of the gun was a rotary bolt operated by a stud that entered a helical cut in the bolt body. The stud in turn was located on the gas piston rod, running below the barrel. This device ensured that, powered by the gases given off from the explosion of the cartridge, the clock-like spiral return spring was rewound and unwound as the bolt was closed. Firing the weapon was simplicity itself. The Lewis gun was loaded using a flat-pan magazine, which was capable of taking either 47 or 97 rounds; spare magazines were carried in special panniers and buckets by the No 2 of the two-man crew.

The Lewis gun was brought out of storage for use with home forces in 1940; a rash of commercial guides were issued that gave simple instruction in how to use the weapon. Its simplicity was a boon to the inexperienced troops as much then as it was in the First World War. Loading the weapon entailed:

1 Making sure the cocking handle was in the forward position;
2 Placing the filed magazine on to the magazine post, pressing down on the magazine while rotating it slightly in both directions until the hook of the catch engaged with the recess in the magazine post;

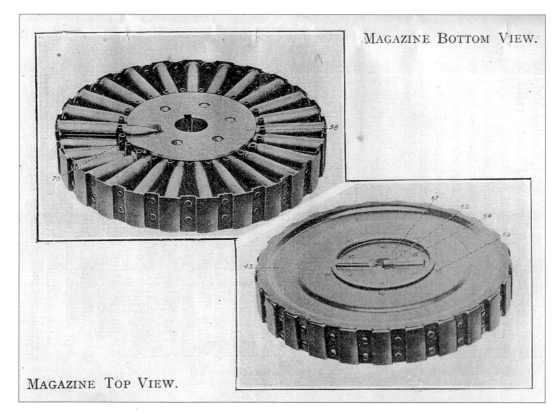

MAGAZINE BOTTOM VIEW.

MAGAZINE TOP VIEW.

LEFT The Lewis gun magazine from the *Machine Gunners Handbook*, 1917.

ABOVE Fitting the magazine to the Lewis gun.

3 Rotating the magazine with the right hand until resistance was met; then
4 Pulling back the cocking handle as far as it would go; this then placed a live round into the cartridge way.

The gun was now ready to fire:

1 When the trigger was pressed, the weapon fired.
2 When pressure on the trigger was released, the cocking handle stopped in the rear position, though the gun was loaded and ready to continue firing.
3 If the trigger pressure was maintained, the gun fired until the magazine was emptied. The cocking handle was then in the forward position; the gun unloaded automatically. The empty magazine rotated freely on the gun.

RIGHT TOP The Lewis gun. Top: loaded and ready to fire. Live round held in position by the Cartridge Guide (44). The Return Spring (10) is held compressed. Middle: Striker (47) has exploded the charge, the bullet (1) is forced down the barrel. Bottom: Bullet has left the barrel, and the cooling system is in operation.

A proportion of the explosive gases have entered the Gas Vent (2) and through the Gas Chamber (3) to the Gas Cylinder (5), thereby forcing the Piston Rod (7) to the rear. The bolt has extracted the Empty Case (23), which is about to be ejected through the ejection slot.

1 Bullet	28 (not used)
2 Gas vent	29 Head of the
3 Gas chamber	ejector
4 Gas regulator	30 Feed arm
5 Gas cylinder	actuating stud
6 Head of the	31 Grooved tail
piston rod	32 Feed arm
7 Piston rod	33 Feed arm pawl
8 Teeth on the	34 Projection
rack	35 Projecting
9 Teeth on the	tongue
pinion	36 Indentations
10 Return spring	37 Separating pegs
11 Striker post	38 Feed arm pawl
12 Cam slot	spring retaining
13 Curved portion	stud
of can slot	39 No 2 (right) stop
14 Bolt	pawl
15 Locking lugs	40 Stop pawl spring
16 Locking	41 Projection
recesses	42 No 1 (left) stop
17 Guide grooves	pawl
18 Bent	43 Top ejector
19 Nose of the sear	44 Cartridge guide
20 Sear	45 Cartridge stop
21 Trigger spring	46 Bullet stop
22 Extractors	47 Striker
23 Empty case	48 Barrel
24 Chamber	mouthpiece
25 (not used)	49 Fore radiator
26 Rear end of the	casing
bolt	50 Flanges of the
27 Tail of the ejector	radiator

RIGHT BOTTOM The action of the Lewis gun in feeding rounds from the magazine into the chamber.

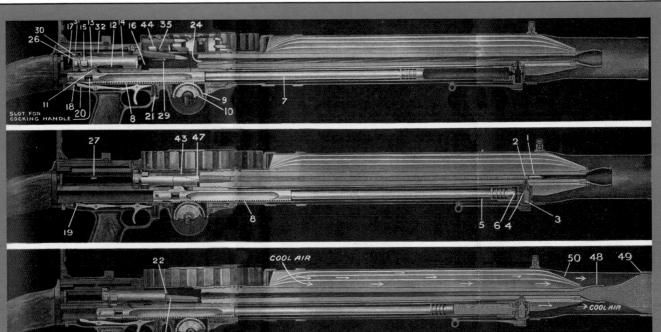

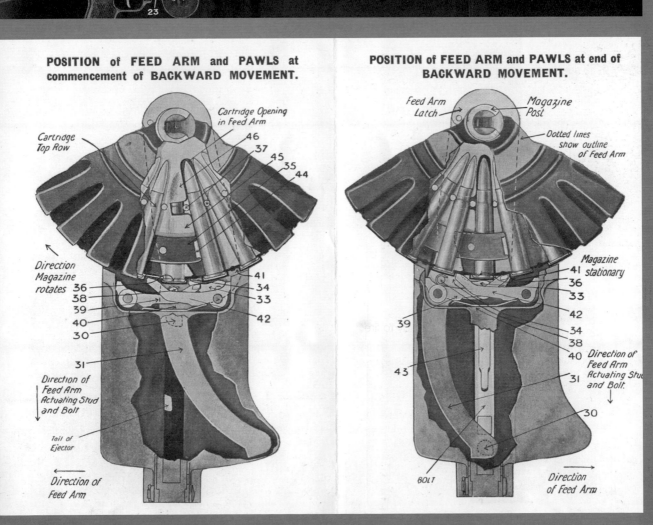

POSITION of FEED ARM and PAWLS at commencement of BACKWARD MOVEMENT.

Cartridge Opening in Feed Arm

Cartridge Top Row

46
37
45
35
44

Direction Magazine rotates

36
38
39
40
30
31

Direction of Feed Arm Actuating Stud and Bolt

Tail of Ejector

Direction of Feed Arm

41
34
33
42

POSITION of FEED ARM and PAWLS at end of BACKWARD MOVEMENT.

Feed Arm Latch

Magazine Post

Dotted lines show outline of Feed Arm

Magazine stationary

41
36
33
42
34
38
40

Direction of Feed Arm Actuating Stud and Bolt

39
43
31
30

BOLT

Direction of Feed Arm

ABOVE Machine gunner proficiency badges: MG, Vickers (or Maxim) machine gunner. LG, Lewis machine gunner.

RIGHT The cap badge of the Machine Gun Corps.

RIGHT Sleeve insignia of trench mortarmen (blue grenade) and bombers (red grenade).

During the First World War, men deemed proficient in handling both Vickers and Lewis machine guns were awarded badges to be worn on the right lower sleeve: MG for machine gunner, LG, for Lewis gunner. In some cases, unofficial, or division-specific machine-gun flashes were also worn on the sleeve. The MGC itself was to wear a cap badge of crossed Vickers machine guns.

If machine guns could provide the infantryman with access to sustained small-arms fire while in the trenches, entry to 'trench artillery' was provided by trench mortars. And it was the trench mortarmen – TMs or 'toc emmas', in the phonetic alphabet of the day – were described as the 'suicide club', a group of soldiers who were as likely as not to be targeted for retaliatory action by their opposite numbers in the opposing trenches. For this reason, among many others, TM men were unpopular in the front line. Trench mortars – simple trench-scale artillery capable of firing high-trajectory shells or bombs – were to become increasing sophisticated as the war proceeded; they were used as a means of destroying or reducing enemy trenches and were capable of killing large numbers of men in any given trenches. The German equivalent – the *minenwerfer* – was especially feared. The British experimented with a variety of contraptions – including catapults firing grenades – but the first effective mortars started to appear in 1915. These included the 'toffee apple' – or 2in medium trench mortar – introduced in mid-1915. It comprised a 42lb spherical bomb containing the explosive charge (ammonal, identified by a pink band, or amatol, a green one) that was mounted on a long shaft. It was fired from a 2in-diameter tube, and was liable to destabilise the round in flight. A single round could destroy 6sq yds of barbed wire.

Perhaps more reliable was the Stokes mortar, a simple 3in drainpipe affair that was effectively the prototype for mortars in use today in armies across the world. Stokes bombs were dropped into the tube, a striker activating the charge and propelling the round up to 1,500yds. Stokes mortar bombs still litter the former battlefields in out of the way places; unstable still, they remain volatile, a deadly echo of a past war. Stokes Toc Emma batteries, organised from 1915, were formed from infantrymen who wore blue flaming grenade sleeve insignia – distinguishing them from battalion bombers, who wore similar, red, grenade badges. Medium and heavy trench mortars were produced from 1916 to 1917, and were manned by artillerymen.

Grenades

As the war progressed, it was the hand grenade – or bomb as it was most commonly referred to – that was largely to replace the rifle as the primary offensive weapon of trench warfare; it required little training to use (although fatal accidents were common), and placed correctly, most grenades had a wide kill radius (defensive grenades) that was more efficient than the well-placed shot of even the most skilled marksman. As the war advanced so did bombing tactics: grenade assaults on front-line trenches were led by 'bayonet men' with the bombers and their grenade carriers following; behind them were 'sandbag men' whose role was to block off sections of trench won in the assault. In this way, front-line trenches were often shared by enemies, with a bomb stop between them – a precarious state of affairs. Later in the war, 'offensive' grenades with a smaller charge that could be used in attacks without danger to the attacker were devised by both sides – the British example being the Type 34.

Nevertheless, despite this sophistication, the British army went to war with an extremely cumbersome grenade – the No 1 grenade. The No 1 was a 16in stick grenade with a cast-iron explosive chamber and streamers to make it stable in flight. As a safety precaution, the No 1 had a cap that was held in place by a safety pin. This cap was intended to protect the percussion fuse, in normal circumstances, not fitted. Bombers had first to rotate the cap to the 'Remove' position, and then taking the cap off the grenade, the fuse was inserted. Replacing the cap, it was set to 'travel'. At this point the bomber could carry the grenade until ready to be thrown; when this point had been reached, the cap was moved on to fire, the safety pin pulled out, and the bomb thrown. The streamers attached to the grenade

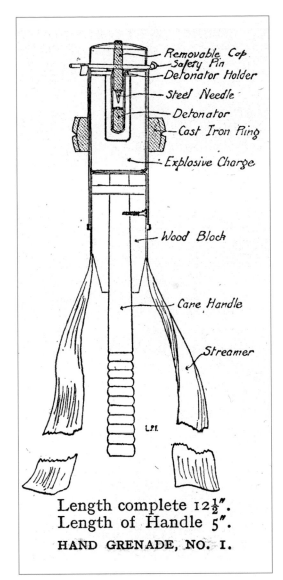

Removable Cap
Safety Pin
Detonator Holder
Steel Needle
Detonator
Cast Iron Ring
Explosive Charge
Wood Block
Cane Handle
Streamer

L.P.I.

Length complete 12½".
Length of Handle 5".
HAND GRENADE, NO. I.

were intended to ensure that it fell head-first – thereby exploding on impact. But it had a fatal flaw – the combination of a long handle and percussion striker – which meant that the bomber had to be extremely careful not to hit the side of the trench when preparing to throw it, a difficult proposition in the confined spaces of the trench. In view of this, the No 1 grenade was updated on 21 May 1915 with a shorter cane or turned wood handle, thereby reducing the length of the grenade to a more manageable length of 12½in.

The need for grenades in front-line service meant that commercial patterns that had hitherto been ignored were now considered viable. As this was the case, the No 2 grenade, sometimes referred to as the 'Hales' after its

NO 2 MARK II GRENADE

From: Handbook on Grenades (1917)

To prepare for use:

1 Holding the grenade downwards, unscrew the back ebonite plug.
2 The detonator is then screwed into the top of the grenade.

To throw:

1 Holding the grenade in the left hand, the streamers are gathered in the palm of the right hand, ensuring that they are free.
2 Holding the handle of the grenade in the right hand, the safety pin is pulled out by the left hand.
3 The grenade is thrown by means of the handle. This is grasped at the furthest point, ie on its grooved portion.
4 The grenade is thrown in an overarm action, by the right hand, making sure that the tail cannot entangle itself with the thrower.
5 The grenade should be thrown well upwards at not less than an angle of about 35 degrees. This increases the range at which the grenade can be thrown, and renders its action more certain by causing it to strike the target nearly vertically. This is especially important when throwing with a following wind.

inventor, or the 'Mexican' after the first armies to take up this pattern, was introduced on 10 October 1914. Similar to the No 1 grenade, it lacked the safety cap, the detonators being inserted into the cap of the grenade just before throwing. The No 2 had a creep spring within the body of the grenade that acted when the cap was forced down upon it on striking the target. Like the No 1 grenade, the No 2 suffered from the length of its throwing handle. However, the No 2 Mark II, with a shortened handle, was introduced early on, thereby reducing the overall length of the grenade from 22in to 12½in – in line with the No 1.

Difficulties of supply, and problems with the ungainly and dangerous nature of these percussion-fused stick grenades meant that by 1915 soldiers were making their own grenades, ignited by a slow-burning fuse – usually at the rate of 1in of fuse per 1.25sec of delay. Typical of these emergency bombs is the 'jam-tin' bomb – literally a tin filled with explosive gun cotton and shrapnel balls – that is particularly associated with the Gallipoli campaign of 1915. The jam tin was formalised into the Nos 8 and 9 grenades, officially produced. Versions of the same grenade, attached to a wooden handle were also developed to improve the throwing distance; other types of 'hair brush' grenade carried blocks of explosive. Another locally made grenade, the Battye bomb – so named after its inventor Major Basil Battye, RE, was manufactured locally at Béthune, and consisted of a cast-iron cylinder containing 40g of explosive, sealed with a wooden stopper and ignited by a Nobel fuse activated by a friction cap. Both this and the jam tins that preceded it were ignited by striking their fuses against a 'friction brassard', a board with a rough surface, just like that of a match box striker, that was worn on the bomber's arm. Both the brassard and the fuse were vulnerable and susceptible to

BELOW Battye bomb.

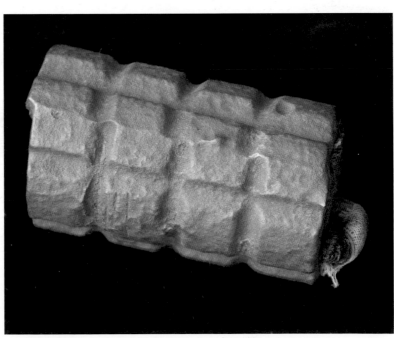

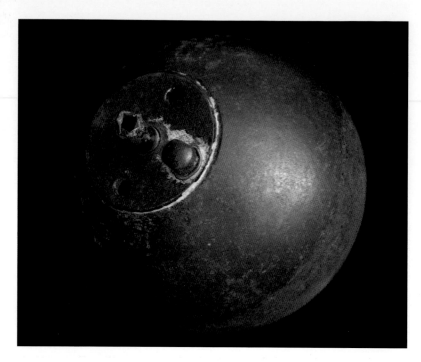

the superior Mills bomb. Resembling a cricket ball, it could be thrown a reasonable distance, but with its simple cast-iron body and cord fuse, it looked particularly archaic. Also ignited by friction, the No 15 was badly affected in wet weather, a factor that was to be a major problem in the Loos campaign of September 1915, the friction brassards issued to bombers becoming useless in the rain. Although half a million grenades of this type were eventually produced, they were unreliable, and were to decline in popularity with the introduction of the Mills bomb in May 1915, named after its principal inventor William Mills.

Officially designated the No 5 grenade, the secret of the success of the Mills bomb lay with its ignition system, which used a striker that was activated when a pin was removed and a lever released; the lever was then ejected and a 4sec fuse activated, during which time the bomber had to throw the grenade. The body of the grenade was formed of cast iron, and weighed 1lb 6½oz; its surface was divided into sections to promote fragmentation. Coloured bands indicated its fillings: pink for ammonal, green for amatol. The grenade's centrepiece contained separate cavities for the striker and the detonator. The striker was kept cocked against a spring, the striker lever holding the striker firmly in position when held against the body of the grenade, locked there by the action of the split safety pin until the bomber removed the pin and threw the grenade. On launching the bomb, the lever flew off, thereby releasing the striker. The impact fired the cap, lighting the safety fuse, and this burned for 5sec before igniting the detonator, which then set off the main charge.

No 5 grenades were supplied in boxes of 12, the central part containing a red tin with the separate igniters, as well as a key to open the base plug of the grenade and access the centrepiece. Each igniter consisted of a cap, cap holder, safety fuse and detonator.

Hand grenades could only be thrown so far; contemporary manuals suggest that the No 5 grenade could be thrown some 35yds by hand. Rifle grenades, at first mistrusted by the War Office but accepted into service at the outbreak of war, could be propelled a greater distance, useful in positional warfare. In many ways the grenade could be considered as the

dampness. These grenades, produced to fill a gap in the supply chain of an important weapon of trench warfare, were unreliable at best.

The No 15 was the first grenade to be mass-produced, again in 1915, intended to fill a gap created by the inadequate supply of

Composition for lighting fuze (Brock Lighter)

Tape

Wire for securing lighter

Wax

Safety fuse

Detonator

Explosive charge

Cast Iron Body

L.P.P.

SECTION

Diameter of Grenade 3″.

BALL HAND GRENADE.

ABOVE, RIGHT AND BELOW The No 5 grenade (Mills bomb), showing filling plug, striker lever, and pin. The grenade retains some of its original paint finish: red filling ring (top) and pink band around the body (ammonal explosive filling).

infantryman's artillery, the rifle grenade being the equivalent of the howitzer. Fired from a rifle loaded with a propellant cartridge (a normal .303 cartridge – minus the bullet – with 35 grains of cordite and a tuft of gun cotton), the No 3 grenade (also known as the Hales, after its inventor) used a steel rod that was placed in the rifle barrel. A percussion grenade, it was filled with the explosive trotyl, or later, amatol or ammonal. An improved version, issued in 1916 (the No 20 grenade), removed some of the complexities of the first pattern – such as a spring clip to grip the rifle muzzle, and a wind vane – but delivered a similar explosive punch.

RIGHT Cross-section of the No 5 grenade.

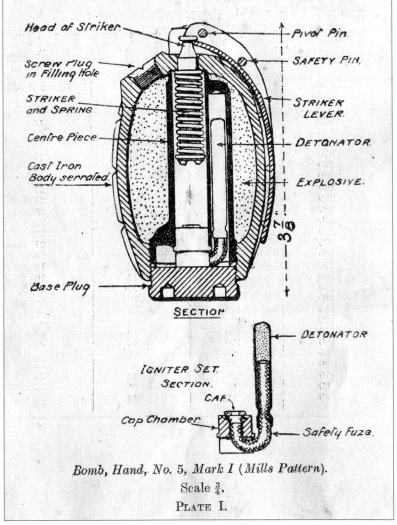

Bomb, Hand, No. 5, Mark I (Mills Pattern).
Scale ¾.
PLATE I.

NO 5 MARK I (HAND) GRENADE

From: *Instructions on Bombing Part 1. British and German Bombs* (1917)

To prepare for use:

1. Unscrew the base and insert the igniter set.
2. Screw home the base with the key provided.

To throw:

1. Hold the bomb in the right hand in such a position that the lever is held securely against the body of the bomb by the fingers.
2. Withdraw the safety pin with the left hand, using a hook if preferred, still keeping a firm grip on the lever.
3. Throw the bomb, using a bowling action.
4. The lever must not be released before the bomb is thrown.

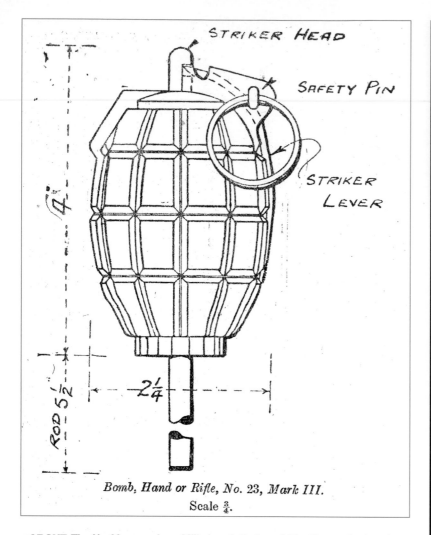

STRIKER HEAD

SAFETY PIN

STRIKER LEVER

4"

ROD 5½"

2¼

Bomb, Hand or Rifle, No. 23, Mark III.
Scale ¾.

ABOVE The No 23 grenade, a Mills bomb that could be thrown by hand, or, fitted with a steel rod, fired as a rifle grenade.

RIGHT The No 36 grenade. This grenade could be thrown by hand or fitted with a gas check disc enabling it to be fired as a rifle grenade from a discharger cup.

NO 36 MARK I GRENADE

From: *Instructions on Bombing Part 1. British and German Bombs* (1917)

Method of use:

1 The bomb is fired from the discharger attached to the rifle. The shock of the discharge is considerable; the rifle must be fired from the kneeling position, with the butt of the rifle resting firmly on the ground.

2 Open the breech of the rifle with the right hand and insert a round of blank ammunition supplied. The breech is then closed and the rifle safety catch is pulled back.

3 The rifle is then turned over so that the magazine is uppermost. Holding the rifle with the left hand at the nose cap, the bomb is inserted, gas check disc first, into the discharger, until the safety pin is level with the rim. The safety pin is then pulled out with the index finger of the right hand, or through the use of a bomber's hook. The bomb is then pushed down into the cup as far as it will go; the cup holds the trigger lever in place.

4 Gripping the rifle firmly with the left hand, above the lower band, it is held at an angle of elevation of around 45 degrees, the heel of the butt resting in a small hole in the ground that had previously been prepared by the heel of the boot.

5 The rifle safety catch is pushed forwards, and the rifle is then fired by pressing on the trigger with the index finger of the right hand, thereby propelling the grenade. In flight, the lever flies off and the fuse is ignited as with the No 5 grenade.

ABOVE No 36 fitted with a gas check disc.

RIGHT The Discharger cup used to propel the No 36 as a rifle grenade.

The No 23 grenade was a new pattern of Mills bomb, initially designed to be used as a rifle grenade, but later (with the Mark II), being adopted either as a hand-thrown bomb or, with the addition of a steel rod screwed into the base plug, a rifle grenade. A special cup was designed to keep the grenade in position for firing, and the bomb itself carried ammonal (marked with a pink band) or amatol (green band). A revised model, the No 36, followed in 1917. The No 36 was first filled with explosive and then dipped in shellac, a process that sealed the grenade and thus prevented rapid deterioration. Unlike its predecessor, the No 36 was fired from a special 'cup discharger', and had a disc-like 'gas check' screwed into its base plate in order to ensure that all the propellant gases did their job. The grenades were packed with a special ballistite cartridge that provided the propellant charge, loaded in the rifle. This charge could propel the grenade some 210yds, six times as far as it could be thrown by hand.

RIGHT No 36 with base plug, igniter set and tool for removing base plug. The gas check disc was screwed into the base plug.

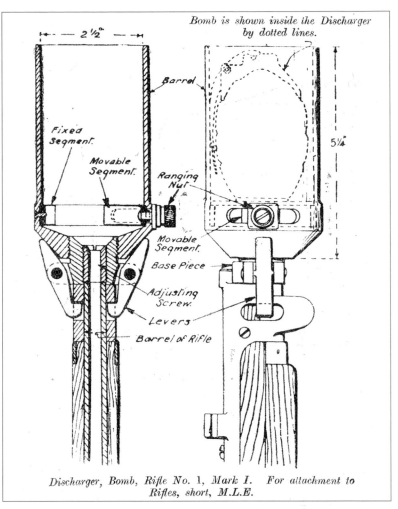

Discharger, Bomb, Rifle No. 1, Mark I. For attachment to Rifles, short, M.L.E.

All Mills bombs were carried in boxes of 12; the detonators were carried separately in a tin in the centre of the box, to avoid unnecessary accidents. Arming the grenade was a tricky business, and required the steady hand of a trained bomber. Battalion bombers were equipped with simple tools to enable them to remove the base plate and prime the grenade; hooks were also provided to bombing specialists to allow them to remove the pins quickly and efficiently, thereby increasing the rate of throw. It has been estimated that approximately 70 million Mills bombs were thrown by the Allies during the war, alongside at least 35 million other types, including many rifle grenades – a testimony to the importance of this weapon in trench combat.

Gas warfare

Gas warfare was to be deployed in an active sense in April 1915, when the Germans first used it in any practical manner during the opening phases of the Second Battle of Ypres. Here, the use of cloud gas was to cause panic and fear among those who faced it, equipped only with wetted handkerchiefs; but the line held, and the use of gas to achieve the much anticipated 'breakthrough' was greatly diminished. From late 1915, with the issue of effective respirators, gas was to become just another weapon to be endured by the man in the trenches. The use of gas on 22 April 1915 by the Germans saw the Allies unprepared. As part of their assault at Ypres, chlorine gas released from cylinders was to overcome the unprotected French troops manning the front line, with between 800 and 1,400 men killed and a further 2–3,000 men injured.

The British first used cloud gas to make good the deficiencies of the artillery preparations for the Battle of Loos, in September 1915. The

LEFT British and German soldiers in respirators, c.1916 (the Germans in 'Gummi masks' and the British in PH helmets).

GAS WARFARE

From: *Knowledge for War. Every Officer's Handbook for the Front* (1916)

The use of poisonous and asphyxiating gases has become an accepted fact in the present war. Every officer, therefore, should be well acquainted with the various ways in which gas is used in the attack.

Two methods are employed in the attack:

1 Emanation
   This method of disseminating gas can only be used in a favourable wind. Its object is to create a poisonous or irritant atmosphere, and this is done either by means of gas forced through tubes in the direction of the enemy, or by means of liquefied gas stored in cylinders under high pressure. The gases used in liquefied form from cylinders are chlorine, mixtures of chlorine and bromine, phosgene gas, sulphureted hydrogen and others.

2 Shells and grenades
   In this method of dissemination shells or bombs are used containing liquid gas or a substance that gives off irritant fumes. Lachrimatory shells causing the eyes to water are also used. Such shells contain bromacetone or chloracetone.

The defence
The best means of learning the defence is to have a thorough knowledge of the attack. Thus the direction of the wind must always be noted, and if favourable for an enemy attack, special observers must be placed to give warning.

chlorine gas – code named 'the accessory' for secrecy – that was to be used in the assault was to be the responsibility of the 'Special Companies' of the Royal Engineers, under the enthusiastic leadership of Major, later Lieutenant Colonel C.H. Foulkes, RE. The original Special Companies were formed in Helfaut, south-east of St Omer, in July 1915, from men with specialist experience transferred from the infantry, and new companies were added right up into September. Those men with suitable experience – often chemistry graduates – were given the rank 'Chemist Corporal'. The Special Companies were distinguished by their multiple vertically striped pink, white and green armbands or brassards – indicating their authority to stay in the trenches during the assault. The gas was dispensed from cylinders fitted with flexible pipes that connected to the business end of the affair, a ½in iron pipe that was up to 10ft long, and which was equipped with a jet at its end. The chlorine was released

RIGHT Sounding the gas alarm, 1915. British troops are depicted wearing early respirators.

ABOVE British troops of the London Rifle Brigade advance through a cloud of poison gas on the opening day of the Battle of Loos, 25 September 1915.

by the Special Company personnel on being given the order to proceed, through the simple act of turning on a stopcock. With the atmospheric conditions indifferent to an effective discharge, the gas did its work only in small parts of the line; elsewhere it had a negative effect on the British troops it was intended to support. Cloud gas release was a crude weapon; by the end of the war gas warfare was more sophisticated, with many means of delivery, in shells, mortars and grenades.

Primitive respirators were improvised in the early days, with General Headquarters of the BEF issuing a directive that field dressings should be soaked in bicarbonate of soda, an alkaline, to combat the suspected chlorine – urine would also be called upon to do the same job. The 1st Canadian Division, on the right flank of the line, were attacked on 24 April, but their protection was only to be wetted handkerchiefs and cotton bandoliers. Scientific advice mustered by the British was to devise a respirator around a pad of cotton waste soaked with sodium hyposulphite, sodium carbonate and glycerine, and was held in black mourning gauze, used to tie the mask to the face. The resulting War Office Black Veiling Respirator was to save many lives in May 1915. It was still

inadequate, however; under pressure of attack, the veiling could not be tied easily, and it only gave protection for a limited period.

A replacement was desperately needed. The first to arrive, in May 1915, was a flannel hood designed by Captain Cluny MacPherson of the Newfoundland Regiment. The hood covered the whole head, its tail being tucked into the tunic to provide a seal. A simple mica window was provided for vision. The 'hypo helmet' (officially, smoke helmet) was soaked in sodium hyposulphite and its wearer given protection by the fact that the 'hypo' solution would counteract the gas drawn in through the material by the process of breathing. In 1915 it was usual for soldiers to carry both the wadding respirator and the hypo helmet in action.

By the autumn of 1915, at the time of Loos, the hypo helmet was replaced by a more sophisticated version, the 'phenate (P) helmet', which used the same basic gas hood design. This was developed in response to the proliferation of gas types, particularly phosgene, ten times more toxic than chlorine. This mask was soaked in sodium phenate, and was made from cotton flannelette (as wool flannel was rotted by the phenate), with two circular glass

THE HYPO HELMET

From: *For Issue to All Ranks. Instructions for use of Respirator and Smoke Helmets June 1915*

RESPIRATORS

1 These are already damped with chemical solution and *should not be wetted*.
2 On the approach of poisonous gases, open the respirator and place the cotton waste pad over the mouth and nose grasping it with the teeth to keep it in position.
3 Now tie off the ends of the veiling behind the head so that the cotton waste closely covers the nose and mouth and pull the free margin of the veiling above the eyebrows to protect the eyes. *Breathe in and out through the mouth only*. After it has been in use for some time, move the respirator to one side or the other so as to breathe through new portions of the cotton waste.
4 When the respirator no longer stops the entrance of gas, apply a fresh one with the same precautions.

SMOKE HELMETS

On the first suspicion of the approach of gas, remove the cap, draw the helmet over the head and *tuck the lower edge of the helmet inside the neck of the frock or shirt by buttoning up the latter*. If the window becomes dim it may be cleaned by gently rubbing against the forehead. Do not damp the helmet.

N.B. – Where both a smoke helmet and a respirator have been issued, *the helmet must be used first* and the respirator held in reserve.

THE PH HELMET

From: *Directions for use & care of tube helmets* (1915)

DESCRIPTION

These Helmets are the same as the 'Smoke Helmet' already issued, except that stronger chemicals are added and a 'Tube-valve' provided through which to breathe out. The Tube-valve makes the helmet cooler and saves the chemicals from being affected by breath. *N.B. Wearer cannot breathe in through the Tube-valve, this is intended for breating out only.*

DIRECTIONS FOR USE

Remove Service Cap. Pull helmet over head. Adjust so that goggles are opposite eyes. Tuck in skirt of helmet so as to close in skirt of helmet. Hold the 'Tube' lightly in lips or teeth like stem of pipe, so as to breathe in past and out through it.

Breathe in through mouth and nose, using the air inside the helmet. Breathe out through tube only.

The valve of the rubber sometimes becomes hard, this can be remedied by breathing out through the valve for about a minute at each helmet inspection, without putting on the helmet.

DIRECTIONS FOR CARE OF TUBE HELMET.

Never use your Tube-helmet for practice or drill. Special helmets are kept in each company for instruction only.

RIGHT The last version of the PH helmet; the PHG, fitted with goggles that were to be held closely to the head, intended to prevent misting. These were mostly issued to artillerymen.

eyepieces, and a tube valve to expel carbon dioxide held in the teeth, with a rubber outlet. This nightmarish creation, also known as the tube helmet, would be famously recorded as the 'goggle-eyed (or googly-eyed) bugger with the tit' by Captains Robert Graves and J.C. Dunn of the Royal Welsh Fusiliers. It would be used, rolled up in readiness on the head, with the hypo helmet in reserve during the disastrous British gas attacks at Loos in September 1915. From January 1916 all P helmets were dipped in hexamine – highly absorbent of phosgene gas – to become the phenate-hexamine or PH helmet. All were clammy, cloying and unpleasant to wear.

The PH helmet could only stop a limited amount of gas, with the likelihood of failure if pushed to its limit by high concentrations of phosgene. In order to improve this situation, Bertram Lambert, a chemistry lecturer at Oxford, developed the concept of layers of lime and sodium permanganate to deal with a range of gases, and this idea was to lead to the development of the Large Box Respirator (LBR) in 1915–16. This used a 'box' of stacked granules of lime-permanganate, pumice soaked in sodium sulphate, and charcoal. The box (actually a converted standard-issue water bottle) was carried in a satchel, and was connected to an impregnated facemask with two eyepieces by a corrugated hose and metal mouthpiece. Large and bulky, it was only to be issued to Royal Engineer gas companies, and soldiers in static positions, such as heavy machine gunners and artillerymen.

The Small Box Respirator (SBR) was developed from its predecessor, in order to provide universal protection from a range of gases, while not being an encumbrance to free movement. Reducing the size of the 'box' was the first step, by modifying its fill – placing the lime-permanganate granules between two

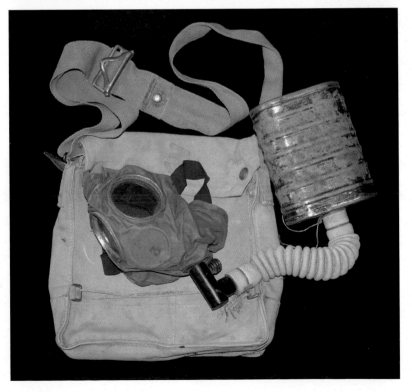

RIGHT The Small Box Respirator (or SBR).

THE SMALL BOX RESPIRATOR (SBR)

From: *Directions for use of Small Box Respirator* (*c*1916)

At ordinary times, the haversack containing the box respirator is to be carried slung over the right shoulder, with the flap fasteners next to the body.

TO CHANGE TO THE ALERT POSITION

1　Pass the left arm backwards through sling so that the haversack hangs in front of the body.
2　Raise the haversack on to the chest by pulling the sling with the left hand until the brass stud on the sling is low enough to button on to the leather tab on the left side of the haversack.
3　Take the coil of whip cord out of the haversack, pass it through the ring pointing to the right of the haversack, round the body, and tie it firmly to the ring pointing to the left of the haversack.

ON THE SOUNDING OF THE GAS ALARM

1　Open the haversack by pulling the cover forward to detach the flap fasteners. **[1]**
2　With the right hand take the mask out of the left compartment of the haversack. **[2]**
3　Grasp the elastics close to the central tape with the thumbs and forefingers of both hands; push the chin well into the mask and pull the elastics over the top of the head *as far as they will go,* ie till the central tape is tight.
4　Holding the metal mouth tube in the right hand outside the mask, push the rubber mouthpiece well into the mouth and draw it forward so that the rubber flange is between the teeth and the lips, and grip the two small rubber projections with the teeth, then start breathing in and out through the tube. **[3]**
5　Open the nose-clip by pinching from outside the circular wire spring below the goggles; push the clip buttons on to the lower part of the nose and release the spring, making sure that the nostrils are closed. **[4]**
6　Complete the fitting of the mask by pulling it well on over the jaw and by smoothing the edge all around the face. **[5]**

7　Do not attempt to speak while wearing the respirator except in case of necessity.
8　If it is necessary to speak, breathe in deeply, grasp the metal tube outside the mask and carefully remove the mouthpiece from between the lips – care being taken not to move the nose-clip.
9　After speaking, immediately replace the mouthpiece and make certain that the nose-clip is properly adjusted.
10　If the eyepieces become dull they can be cleaned by inserting the thumbs into the pockets alongside the goggles and wiping the inside of the windows.
11　If the nose-clip slips off, replace it at once.
12　After use, carefully dry the mouthpiece and eye rims from the inside and also inside surface of the mask, so as to remove the condensed moisture resulting from the breath.

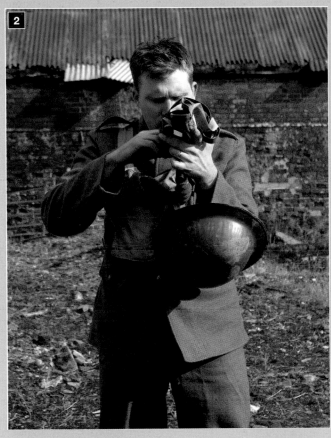

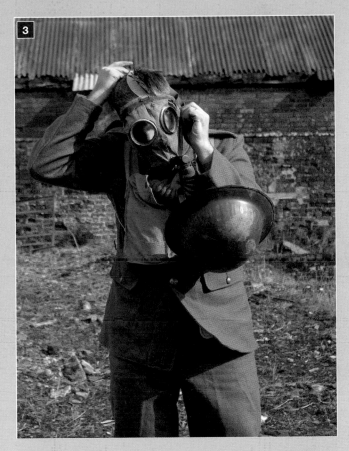

layers of charcoal. Other improvements were an exhalation valve (which also had a device to drain saliva), and a haversack that could be worn either slung over the shoulder or, through the use of a lug and leather strap, could be hitched up on to the chest (strap over the head) into the 'alert' position. The facemask was issued in four sizes, its number stamped on the mask and on the haversack. When worn, the soldier would grip the inner rubber mouthpiece between his teeth, and use the integrated nose clip to ensure his breathing was through the 'box'. When first issued in August–October 1916, the masks were individually fitted, and each soldier was acclimatised by exposure (while wearing the mask) in a tear-gas chamber for five minutes. This mask was to prove highly effective.

With the advent of gas as a weapon of war, some means of alerting the men in the front lines was necessary. From the early days, the army relied upon any number of extemporised warnings including, typically, shell cases suspended from the trench sides,

or from simple tripods near gun sites. Ordinary gas gongs had the advantage that the material from which they were constructed was readily available, and needed little more than the ability to suspend the gong upside down, and the provision of an appropriate piece of metal or wood to beat the gong with. Rattles had been used by the police in Victorian Britain before they were given whistles, and in 1917, the BEF was to issue them as an efficient means of gas warning. Rattles had the advantage that if swung with sufficient vigour, they could be heard from some distance; in 1917 they were replaced by an even more efficient tool, an air-powered horn – known as a Strombos horn – the sound of which could carry for at least 20 miles.

Trench raids

Not every attack staged on the Western Front would be a major one; trench raids were more often than not a significant means of establishing control over the battlefront, or simply a means of gaining intelligence of who exactly was occupying the trenches opposite. Capturing prisoners who could be interrogated, or even just the gathering of insignia from dead soldiers, was deemed important for intelligence purposes, and trench raids were intended to furnish this. Raids varied from minor affairs with small groups of men, to larger ones involving artillery preparation. In all cases, grenades would be the most significant weapons, as would a variety of extemporised weapons that had close links with medieval warfare.

Trench raids were considered by the High Command to be an operational necessity, required for at least two reasons: to provide information on the enemy in the trenches ahead; and to maintain the offensive spirit. Common throughout the war, but increasingly from 1915, were trench raids at night; everything from single officers exploring no-man's-land, to organised miniature offensives protected by complex artillery box barrages. In all cases, the objectives were limited and definite.

Trench raids in most cases required stealth and were usually carried out by volunteers who were trained to move forward into no-man's-

BELOW Australian infantry wearing Small Box Respirators, c.1917.

TRENCH RAIDS

From: *Notes on Minor Enterprises* (1916)

Success in a minor operation against the enemy's trenches depends mainly on careful selection and reconnaissance of the objective and on a thorough working out of all the details beforehand.

The selection and reconnaissance of the objective, as well as the concealment of our intentions, can only be carried out successfully, if superiority in patrol work between the lines has been established.

The number of men employed varies according to the nature and extent of the objective. The German trenches have been entered by patrols of from 2 to 8 men for the purpose of securing an identification, or obtaining information on some definite point, eg the existence of a suspected mine shaft. Raids on the enemy's trenches have been made by parties varying from 80 to 800 men, with or without the cooperation of the artillery.

DRESS ARMS AND EQUIPMENT IN TRENCH RAIDS

From: *Notes on Minor Enterprises* (1916)

A All identification marks, or badges on the uniform, and all identity discs should be removed to prevent the enemy obtaining any useful information.

B Men's faces and hands should be darkened.

C Khaki woollen caps or Balaclava helmets are suitable head-dress. Woollen gloves to be worn while crawling forward and thrown away on reaching the enemy's parapet have been found useful.

D Men should be armed according to the tasks they are to perform. Bayonet men should carry rifles and bayonets and 50 rounds of ammunition.

E Revolvers, knobkerries and daggers have been used.

F Electric torches fixed to the rifle with black insulating tape have been found useful for men detailed to clear dugouts.

G The raiding party should be provided with the most powerful wire cutters available. Men for wire cutting should be provided with leather hedging gloves.

H In addition to the grenadiers, every man should carry two grenades.

BELOW Trench club 'Knobkerries' and 'nail' trench knife.

land with the least disturbance, cutting wire as silently as possible, and maintaining a low profile in case of star shells or sweeping machine-gun fire. Typically, raids involved dropping into the enemy trenches in order to gather intelligence: the state of the opposing trenches; the collection of unusual patterns of grenades; the gathering of enemy pay books and other means of identifying the unit occupying the trenches, including the taking of prisoners; and the location of machine guns, gas cylinders and other equipment that could be destroyed at a later date by an artillery bombardment. For the assaulting soldiers, attention to detail was essential.

Of all the items associated with trench warfare, the rediscovery of clubs and knives as weapons are identified with the descent of warfare from the ideal of open battle, to the extended and stalemated nightmare of the trenches. Of all weapons, clubs have an ancestry that extends back millennia. In the strict confines of the trench, rifles with fixed bayonets could not be wielded effectively, and where a modicum of surprise was needed, the club, knife, revolver and grenade found favour in night trench raids. In most cases, clubs and knives were fashioned from whatever was to hand – made both by soldiers themselves and in the workshops of the Army Ordnance Corps. Typical clubs – often referred to as 'knobkerries' – had a long turned-wood handle studded with boot cleats; other examples of these have nails instead of cleats. Other versions were probably improvised in the trenches, or even at home and sent to the front.

In most cases, the standard British 1907-pattern bayonet was too long to be of any effective use in trench raids. As no official knives were to be issued to British troops, home-made examples were actively employed. It has been suggested that the knife was not a preferred weapon on British trench raids; using a bayonet on the end of a rifle as trained was one thing, but getting close enough to stab a man with a knife was quite another. The trench club was a more commonly used weapon. While other nations were issued with short knives for battle use, the British soldier resorted to privately purchased examples or to manufacturing his own, close to the front line. Typical of this industry was the use of cut-down bayonets

TRENCH KNIVES

Most British trench knives were constructed in the field using whatever materials were available; sharpened metal files, barbed-wire pickets and cut-down bayonets were commonplace. But in answer to the need for suitable trench weapons, commercial companies soon got in on the act. The Robbins-Dudley Company of Dudley was one of the first to respond to the demand, designing a number of daggers and 'push-knives' for trench use that for the most part were bought by officers. The Robbins-Dudley 'punch knife' was a fearsome weapon that was based on an aluminium handle with a 3½in heat-treated steel dagger blade, housed in a leather sheath.

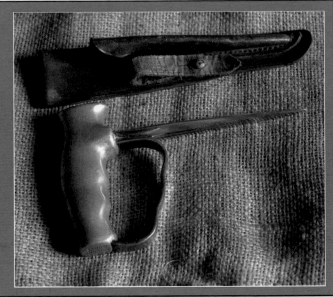

RIGHT Robbins 'push dagger'.

– the Canadian Ross bayonet (for the ill-fated Ross Rifle, withdrawn as being unfit for front-line service in late 1916), already relatively short, was a favourite, but any other suitable piece of metal that would carry a blade was also to be pressed into service.

Over the top

For the infantryman, going 'over the top' or 'over the bags' was, relatively speaking, a rare event. The large set-piece battles so commonly associated with the First World War

BELOW 'Over the top', a staged picture of soldiers leaving an open trench.

took a considerable amount of planning, with extended periods of artillery preparation and the gathering of reinforcements in the rear areas, clogging transport arteries and communication trenches. Nevertheless, at some point most infantry soldiers would experience the terror of rising out of the trenches in broad daylight to face the enemy that they had previously only caught fleeting glimpses of through trench periscopes, and the resulting battles have been the focus for heated discussion over the decades since the end of the war.

Artillery was a key component of all attacks; massing guns and having sufficient ammunition to subdue the enemy became essential if an attack was to succeed. For the British, supply of guns and ammunition took some time to catch up with the ambitions of the General Staff, and in early 1915 the inadequacy of the supply led to the fall of the Liberal government during the 'shell crisis'. With inadequate ammunition to support the offensives of Neuve Chappelle and Fromelles, the German defences

were intact, the barbed wire uncut. Adequate supplies would have to await the work of the newly formed Ministry of Munitions in mobilising effort on the home front. Nevertheless, the effects of pre-battle bombardments were impressive, even in 1915.

But it was the Battle of the Somme in 1916, the first major British offensive on the Western Front since Loos in September 1915, which was to demonstrate the power of artillery. The bombardment of the German lines that opened on 24 June 1916 and lasted until zero hour on 1 July, became known as *trommelfeuer*: drumfire. Intended to destroy enemy batteries, trenches, dugouts and barbed wire, the bombardment involved ceaseless shelling from almost 1,500 guns and howitzers of all types firing some 1.7 million rounds. But even this level of fire was inadequate for a front of 18 miles. The men who went 'over the top' at 7.30am, zero hour, on 1 July 1916, climbed over the sandbag parapet to face the German survivors of the barrage, ready to meet them.

In all battles, at zero hour, soldiers experienced the terror of rising from their trenches to face the unknown, the practicality achieved through trench ladders, more often than not duckboards with some of the slats removed to allow the boots to fit. Putting these in place would remind the soldiers of their coming responsibilities. Coordinating the attack were the subalterns, junior officers in charge of platoons who would face the dangers of no-man's-land with their NCOs and men – often conspicuous with their Sam Browne belts and distinctive open-necked uniform. With officers in their distinctive garb often targeted by the enemy, it is understandable that some would adopt the dress of the ordinary soldier, with discreet rank badges carried on the shoulder straps of an ordinary 'Tommy's' tunic.

Equipped with whistles, wristwatches and the hefty Mark VI Webley revolver – first issued in 1915 and capable of stopping any man with its powerful .455-calibre bullet – it would be these officers who would signify the attack in

ASSAULT EQUIPMENT

From: *Notes for Infantry Officers on Trench Warfare* (1916)

Assaulting troops should be as lightly equipped as possible, but it is difficult to reduce the weight carried below the following scale (carried in addition to battle order webbing/leather equipment, steel helmet and rifle):

200 rounds Small Arms Ammunition (SAA)
One day's rations (in addition to iron rations)
Two sandbags (for constructing defences)
One pick or shovel to every third man (for 'turning trenches')

Extra wire cutters, flares, smoke candles, etc, will be carried by a proportion of the men. Grenadiers carry rifle and bayonet and 50 rounds SAA.

BELOW Ready to go over top. A patrol prepares to raid German trenches.

RIGHT Preparing to go 'over the top'.

the eerie silence that followed the end of the bombardment. It is not surprising then, that the whistle has entered into the mythology of the war. Most were made by the famous firm of Hudson's, in Birmingham, the manufacturer of 'The Metropolitan' police whistle and its military versions since the mid-part of the 19th century. Yet whistles were employed on other tasks: warning of gas attacks, for instance, or, more usually, by day sentries keeping watch through periscopes for incoming 'minies' – *minenwerfer* trench mortars. Easily spotted in flight, sentries would blow their whistles and shout 'minies to the left or right' as appropriate.

With zero hour imminent, and the bombardment reaching its height, soldiers would hope that the enemy would be stunned into submission, and be forced to keep their heads down – rather than pouring fire into the oncoming ranks of soldiers as they left the safety of their trenches. But in reality, as they stumbled forward over no-man's-land, soldiers would be pushed into a maelstrom of machine-gun fire, counter bombardment and the broken landscape of the modern battlefield. Overhead,

was the continuing barrage that was intended to protect the attackers, a moving curtain of shellfire that would attempt to clear the trenches in front of the living wave of men. But the battlefield would change over the course of the war, with tanks and aircraft taking their places alongside the infantryman in the coordinated, all-arms attacks of 1918. Most men would find it disorienting, and getting into the enemy's trenches was a terrifying experience.

Once in the enemy trenches, bombing parties would ensure that they were cleared. In front of the bombers were bayonet men, picking their way around the traverses. Behind them were the bombers, trained in the use of grenades and ensuring that dugouts gained their special attention. Following them there were the 'sandbag' men, trained in consolidation. Carrying spades and filling sandbags brought over by every infantryman, they worked to secure the captured trench, and to put in place blocks to prevent reinforcement by the enemy along the trench system. Many a trench captured in this way would be shared between opposing forces, assimilated into

LEFT RAMC medics attend to wounded in a service trench.

front-line systems, yet still in possession of both sides. Counter-attacks would follow, and often would succeed; it all depended upon the artillery support, the number of reinforcements, and the capabilities of supply over the now heavily cut up no-man's-land.

The aftermath of an attack would be the suffering of men, many of whom would be stranded in no-man's-land, sheltering in shell holes, waiting and hoping for the arrival of stretcher-bearers. Stretcher-bearers were battalion men who gave up their arms to carry their stretcher, the bearing of arms by medics being expressly forbidden in war. Ideally, at least six men would be needed per stretcher; this was not always achievable, and German prisoners were often drafted in to carry wounded soldiers back, as it was an offence under King's Regulations to escort wounded soldiers back without the express permission of an officer. Regimental stretcher-bearers

ABOVE AND BELOW Stretcher bearer at his stretcher bearer's station close to the frontline.

DUTIES OF REGIMENTAL STRETCHER-BEARERS

From: *Field Service Regulations Part II Organisation and Administration, 1909*, (reprinted with amendments 1914)

A When an action begins, the regimental stretcher-bearers, without their arms, will be placed under the medical officer's orders. Stretchers and stretcher-bearers' armlets (to be worn on the left arm in lieu of the Red Cross brassard) form part of the medical equipment.

B The duties of the regimental medical establishments in action are:

(i) To afford first aid to the wounded.

(ii) To carry cases not able to walk over to the nearest and most suitable cover.

(iii) To throw up some sort of cover to protect serious cases that cannot be moved.

(iv) To assist the medical units after an action, if required, and if available.

The first field dressing applied as a protection against dirt and to stop haemorrhage, with the addition of some support to a broken limb, before removal of the patient, is all that is needed on the field itself. After this first aid, a wounded man should be left where he lies, under as good cover as possible, unless the nature of the ground, a pause in the fighting, or the approach of darkness allows systematic collection and removal.

wore a brassard or armband bearing the initials 'SB'. Many were bandsmen, others were infantrymen detailed for the job – a dangerous task, requiring service under fire, usually in no-man's-land.

Regimental stretcher-bearers' responsibilities ended at the Regimental Aid Post (RAP); from here men would be dispatched to the rear areas and would be in the care of the Royal Army Medical Corps (RAMC), men who wore the red Geneva Cross armbands, and the trade badge of the medical orderly – again a red Geneva Cross – whose role it was (as part of the Army Medical Services) to care for the wounded and to evacuate them efficiently from the front line to a further destination, hoped for by most soldiers as being 'Blighty'. Movement from the front was long, laborious and for the wounded, painful. The chain was a long one: first to the RAP, run by a RAMC doctor and small number of orderlies that was set up close to the front line and adjacent to Battalion Headquarters (usually in dugouts or ruined buildings). Next in the chain was the Advanced Dressing Station (ADS), set up at the furthest limit of wheeled transport to the front, and run by the RAMC Field Ambulance, with three such units of men attached to an infantry division.

In the First World War, the rate and scale of casualties is still breathtaking: infamously, the opening hour of the Battle of the Somme on 1 July 1916 saw at least 50,000 men killed, wounded or reported missing. Some 10–15% of soldiers mobilised were killed, but many more were wounded or taken prisoner, and it was relatively rare for a front-line soldier to survive the war completely unscathed. Injuries were a common experience; most longed for a minor wound that would take them back home to 'Blighty'; not everyone would have the opportunity.

BELOW A wounded soldier is given a sip of water by a medical officer.

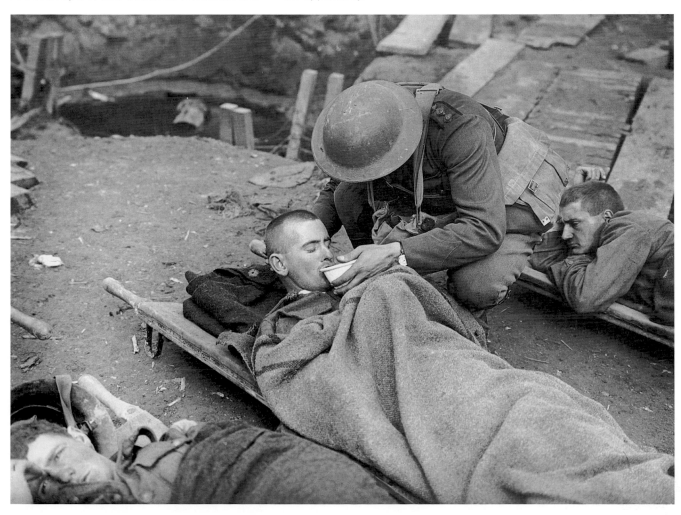

Postscript

Demobilised

The Armistice with Germany came into effect at 11.00am on 11 November 1918. Though men lost their lives on this day, and many more would suffer from their wounds and become casualties of the influenza epidemic, the majority returned home. Yet with so many demobilised, unemployment was rife, and the dream of a 'land fit for heroes' very quickly dissipated

OPPOSITE Poppies as reminders of battle on the fields of the Somme.

RIGHT Private
J.T. Robinson of
Belford enlisted in
the Northumberland
Fusiliers in November
1915. John Robinson
was transferred
to the 1/5th West
Riding Regiment on 4
September 1916, the
day after the battalion
had suffered heavy
casualties at Thiepval
on the Somme. He
was wounded a year
after joining, and was
discharged from the
army in March 1917.
The village of Belford
commemorated his
service with this
certificate.

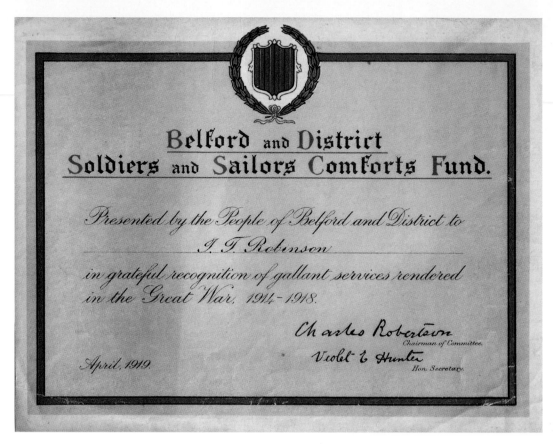

Belford and District
Soldiers and Sailors Comforts Fund.

Presented by the People of Belford and District to

J. T. Robinson

*in grateful recognition of gallant services rendered
in the Great War, 1914–1918.*

Charles Robertson
Chairman of Committee.

April, 1919.

Violet E Hunter
Hon. Secretary.

The war officially ended with the armistice of 11 November 1918. The Allied armies had dealt a succession of hammer blows on the Germans since the opening of the Battle of Amiens on 8 August 1918 – the beginning of one hundred days of continuous advance. With heavy irony, the British found themselves back where they had started from, the Germans pushed in retreat to a line that was broadly similar to the one where they had first met the British 'Old Contemptibles' four years before. With the armistice agreed, the war on the Western Front ended abruptly. Its terms required the cessation of hostilities at 11.00am on 11 November 1918, together with the evacuation of occupied territory, the surrender of large quantities of arms and equipment, and the disarming and internment of the High Seas Fleet. German soil was to be occupied west of the Rhine, and the British army moved into Germany on 17 November.

For those troops not instructed to take on occupation duties, release from the army could not come soon enough. For a lucky few, demobilisation was available from the end of November, but many more would have to wait some time for their exoneration from service. While skilled men vital for the rebuilding of Britain's peacetime industry were released first, with around 2,750,00 men processed by August 1919, the procedure would not be complete until as late as 1922. Men leaving the army were allowed to keep their greatcoat and boots, and were issued either with an allowance for new clothes, or a 'demob' suit. Any arrears owed were paid, a travel pass was given out, as was a guarantee of unemployment benefit of up to 24 shillings a week, the allowance to last 12 months. Despite their release, the army was at pains to point out that each soldier was transferred to the reserves – in case hostilities should return.

Many more personnel would be seriously wounded, maimed or psychologically damaged – for these men, adjusting back to family life after the war would be a struggle. Serious wounds or disability led to soldiers being discharged from the service, receiving a war pension and a silver war badge. Some 2,414,000 men were entitled to a war pension, the scale of which varied according to the severity of the injury or other service-related condition, and the resulting disability. From 1917 there was an acceptance that psychological damage – termed 'shell shock' as early as 1915 – would be grounds for a discharge. In all cases, the maximum pension they could hope to receive was 25 shillings a week. The silver war badge these men wore was the visible evidence that a serviceman had served his country honourably, and through sickness or wounding had been released from service.

In fact, the soldiers of the First World War had little to show for their efforts: a simple bronze star if they had served in the early part of the war, with just two simple awards, the War Medal and Victory Medal, from 1916. Commonplace, these medals became known as 'Pip, Squeak and Wilfred', named after three comic-strip characters. There was irony in the name. In the hard times of the 1920s and 1930s, old soldiers down on their luck would find that these hard-won items would have little intrinsic value, difficult to pawn. Gallantry medals would have greater value.

The British Empire had seen over 947,000 men killed, and 2,121,906 men wounded. In all, at least 10–15% of those who joined up were killed. The next of kin of those who had given their lives received a bronze memorial disc with the name of the serviceman worked in relief. Mass production of the plaques commenced in December 1918, and a total number of around 1,150,000 were produced for all those who had died from war-related causes. Yet one of the many tragedies of the First World War was the influenza pandemic of 1918, among its victims otherwise healthy adults who had come through the war unharmed. For soldiers to lose their lives from a case of the flu in this way was yet another sad irony.

For those who survived, soldiers returned from the war in 1918–19 expecting a 'land fit for heroes to live in' – the now clichéd phrase first used by David Lloyd George in campaigning during the 'coupon' or 'khaki' election of December 1918. He was to remain as prime minister, a post he had held since 1916, when he replaced Asquith. Yet delivering this ideal would not be easy. With so many servicemen demobilised, and in the depth of a post-war slump following the gearing-up of a nation for 'total war', finding employment was a nightmare task. After all the empty promises, charity, and the sale of small goods, would be the only way for many of scratching a living in the cold, post-war world, the long struggle of many ex-servicemen to find employment a national disgrace.

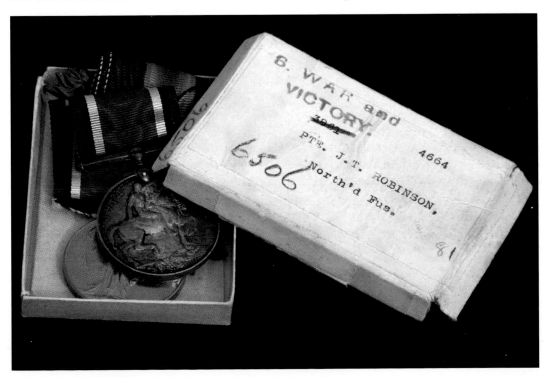

LEFT Private John Robinson's war medals were never worn or removed from their original box of issue. Serving in France from 1916, he was entitled to the British War Medal and Victory Medal, the pair nick-named 'Mutt and Jeff'; those soldiers serving overseas received the 1914–15 Star in addition – forming a trio known as 'Pip, Squeak and Wilfred'.

Selected sources and reading

Official manuals

General Staff, 1908. *Military Engineering (Part 1) Field Defences, 1908*. HMSO.
General Staff, 1911. *Manual of Field Engineering, 1911* (reprinted 1913). HMSO.
General Staff, 1914. *Field Service Pocket Book*. HMSO.
General Staff, 1914. *Field Service Regulations Part I. Operations, 1909* (reprinted with amendments 1914). HMSO.
General Staff, 1914. *Field Service Regulations Part II. Organisation and Administration, 1909* (reprinted with amendments 1914). HMSO.
General Staff, 1914. *Musketry Regulations Part I, 1909* (reprinted with amendments 1914). HMSO.
General Staff, 1914. *Musketry Regulations Part II (Rifle Ranges and Musketry Appliances), 1909* (reprinted with amendments 1914). HMSO.
General Staff, 1914. *Infantry Training (4-Company Organisation), 1909* (reprinted with amendments 1914). HMSO.
General Staff, 1915. *Notes from the Front, Part 3, 1915*. HMSO.
General Staff, 1916. *Notes on Minor Enterprises, March 1916*. HMSO.
General Staff, 1916. *Notes on Trench Warfare for Infantry Officers, March 1916*. HMSO.
General Staff, 1917. *Infantry Machine-Gun Company Training (Provisional), 1917*. HMSO.
General Staff, 1917. *Instructions on Bombing Part 1. British and German Bombs*. HMSO.
General Staff, 1917. *Instructions for the Training of Platoons for Offensive Action, 1917*. HMSO.
General Staff, 1917. *Method of Instruction in the Lewis Gun*. HMSO.
General Staff, 1917. *Notes on Trench Warfare for Infantry Officers. Revised Diagrams. December 1916*. HMSO.
General Staff, 1917. *A Sequence of Musketry Training* (1915, reprinted with amendments). HMSO.
General Staff, 1918. *Bayonet Training, 1918* (reprinted with amendments 1916). HMSO.
General Staff, 1918. *The Employment of Machine Guns*. HMSO.
General Staff, 1918. *Notes for Instructors on the Use of the Rifle*. HMSO.
War Office, 1904. *Fitting and Wearing the Equipment, Bandolier, Pattern 1903*. HMSO.
War Office, 1912. *Manual of Elementary Military Hygiene* (reprinted 1914). HMSO.
War Office, 1913. *The Pattern 1908 Web Infantry Equipment*. HMSO.
War Office, 1914. *Clothing Regulations, Part 1 Regular Forces, 1914*. HMSO.
War Office, 1914. *Field Service Manual Infantry Battalion (Expeditionary Force)*. HMSO.
War Office, 1914. *Manual of Physical Training, 1908* (reprinted with amendments published in army orders to 1 December 1914). HMSO.
War Office, 1915. *Bayonet Fighting. Instruction with Service Rifle and Bayonet, 1917*. HMSO.
War Office, 1915. *Handbook for the .303-in Vickers Machine Gun (Magazine Rifle Chamber) Mounted on Tripod Mounting, Mark IV*. HMSO.
War Office, 1915 *The Pattern 1915 Leather Infantry Equipment*. HMSO.
War Office, 1915. *Treatise on Ammunition,* 10th Edition. HMSO.
War Office, 1917. *Field Almanac, 1917*. HMSO.

Commercial manuals and guides

Ainslie, Major G.M., *Hand Grenades. A Handbook on Rifle and Hand Grenades* (Chapman & Hall, 1917).

'An Adjutant', *Squad, Section, and Company Drill Made Easy, in accordance with Infantry Training, 1911* (Gale & Polden, 1914).

Anon., *Guide for the .303 Vickers Machine Gun. Its Mechanism and Drill with Questions & Answers* (Gale & Polden, 1915).

Anon., *What Every Soldier Ought to Know. Compiled from Official Manuals* (Oxford University Press, 1915).

Anon., *Rank at a Glance* (George Philip & Son, 1915).

Anon., *Badges and their Meaning* (George Philip & Son, 1916).

Baden-Powell, Sir Robert, *Quick Training for War* (Herbert Jenkins, 1914).

Bostock, J. Lieutenant, *The Machine Gunner's Handbook*, 11th edition (W.H. Smith & Son, 1917).

Lake, Captain B.C., *Knowledge for War. Every Officer's Handbook for the Front* (Harrison & Sons, 1916).

Pridham, Major C.H.B., *Lewis Gun Mechanism Made Easy* (Gale & Polden, 1940).

'Second in Command', *Notes on Trench Routine & Discipline* (Forster Groom & Co, 1916).

Solano, Captain E.J. (ed), *Physical Training (Senior Course).* Imperial Army Series, based on official manuals (John Murray, 1913).

Solano, Captain E.J. (ed), *Drill and Field Training.* Imperial Army Series, based on official manuals (John Murray, 1914).

Solano, Captain E.J. (ed), *Camps, Billets, Cooking, Ceremonial.* Imperial Army Series, based on official manuals (John Murray, 1915).

Solano, Captain E.J. (ed), *Field Entrenchments, Spadework for Riflemen.* Imperial Army Series, based on official manuals (John Murray, 1915).

Solano, Captain E.J. (ed), *Musketry (.303 and .22 Cartridges).* Imperial Army Series, based on official manuals (John Murray, 1916).

Vickers Armstrong Limited, *Handbook of the Vickers Machine Gun (Water Cooled) for Land Service.* (Vickers Armstrong Ltd).

Other sources

Bodsworth, J., *British Uniforms and Equipment of the Great War, 1914–18* (MLRS, 2010).

Brayley, M.J., *Bayonets: An Illustrated History* (David & Charles, 2004).

Brayley, M.J., *British Web Equipment of the Two World Wars* (Crowood, 2005).

Bull, S. (ed), *An Officer's Manual of the Western Front* (Conway, 2008).

Chambers, S.J., *Uniforms & Equipment of the British Army in World War 1. A Study in Period Photographs* (Schiffer, 2005).

Dixey, W.A., 'On the design, details of construction, and use of trench periscopes', *Transactions of the Optical Society*, vol. 15, 78–98, 1915.

Doyle, P. and Foster, C., *British Army Cap Badges of the First World War* (Shire, 2011).

Edwards, D. and Langley, D., *British Army Proficiency Badges* (Wardley Publishing, 2005).

Haselgrove, M.J. and Radovic, B., *Helmets of the First World War, Germany, Britain and their Allies* (Schiffer, 2000).

Haselgrove, M.J. and Radovic, B., *The History of the Steel Helmet in the First World War. Volume Two, Great Britain, Greece, Holland, Italy, Japan, Poland, Portugal, Romania, Russia, Serbia, Turkey, United States* (Schiffer, 2006).

Holmes, R., *Tommy. The British Soldier on the Western Front 1914–1918* (HarperCollins, 2004).

Landers, R., *'Grenade' British and Commonwealth Hand and Rifle Grenades* (Landers Publishing, 2001).

Pegler, M., *The Lee-Enfield Rifle* (Osprey, 2012).

Saunders, A., *Weapons of the Trench War 1914–18* (Sutton, 1999).

Saunders, A., *Dominating the Enemy, War in the Trenches 1914–1918* (Sutton, 2000).

Shipley, A,E., *The Minor Horrors of War.* (Smith Elder & Co, 1915).

Skennerton, I., *The British Service Lee* (Arms & Armour Press, 1982).

Wheeler–Holohan, V., *Divisional and Other Signs* (John Murray, 1920).

Blanco and Bull: http://www.blancoandbull.com
Karkee Web: http://www.karkeeweb.com/index.html#home
Long, Long, Trail: http://www.1914-1918.net

Index